Rosary Primer

Rosary Primer

The Prayers, The Mysteries,
and The New Testament

Mark G. Boyer

WIPF & STOCK · Eugene, Oregon

ROSARY PRIMER
The Prayers, The Mysteries, and The New Testament

Copyright © 2018 Mark G. Boyer. All rights reserved. Except for brief quotations in critical publications or reviews, no part of this book may be reproduced in any manner without prior written permission from the publisher. Write: Permissions, Wipf and Stock Publishers, 199 W. 8th Ave., Suite 3, Eugene, OR 97401.

Wipf & Stock
An Imprint of Wipf and Stock Publishers
199 W. 8th Ave., Suite 3
Eugene, OR 97401

www.wipfandstock.com

PAPERBACK ISBN: 978-1-5326-4870-0
HARDCOVER ISBN: 978-1-5326-4871-7
EBOOK ISBN: 978-1-5326-4872-4

Manufactured in the U.S.A.

Dedicated to
past and present members of
St. Joachim Parish,
Old Mines, Missouri,
first to nourish my faith.

Contents

The Christian Bible (New Testament) | ix
Introduction | xi
  Rosary Primer | xii
  How to Pray the Rosary | xiii
  The Mysteries | xvii
  This Book | xviii

1. The Joyful Mysteries | 1
    The Annunciation | 2
    The Visitation | 7
    The Nativity | 12
    The Presentation | 17
    The Finding of Jesus in the Temple | 23

2. The Luminous Mysteries | 29
    Baptism in the Jordan | 30
    The Wedding at Cana | 35
    Proclamation of the Kingdom of God | 40
    The Transfiguration | 46
    Institution of the Eucharist | 51

3. The Sorrowful Mysteries | 57
    The Agony in the Garden | 58
    The Scourging at the Pillar | 63
    The Crowning with Thorns | 68
    The Carrying of the Cross | 73
    The Crucifixion | 78

Contents

4. The Glorious Mysteries | 84
   The Resurrection | 85
   The Ascension | 90
   The Descent of the Holy Spirit Upon the Apostles | 95
   The Assumption | 100
   The Coronation of the Blessed Virgin Mary | 106

Bibliography | 117
Recent Books by Mark G. Boyer | 119

The Christian Bible
(New Testament)

Abbreviations

Acts	Acts of the Apostles
Col	Letter to the Colossians
1 Cor	First Letter of Paul to the Corinthians
Gal	Letter of Paul to the Galatians
Heb	Letter to the Hebrews
John	John's Gospel
Luke	Luke's Gospel
Mark	Mark's Gospel
Matt	Matthew's Gospel
2 Pet	Second Letter of Peter
Rev	Revelation
Rom	Letter of Paul to the Romans

Notes

The Christian Bible, consisting of twenty-seven named books, is also called the New Testament; it is accepted by Christians as Holy Scripture.

In notating biblical texts, the first number refers to the chapter in the book, and the second number refers to the verse within the chapter. Thus, Mark 6:2 means that the quotation comes from Mark's Gospel, chapter 6, verse 2. When more than one sentence appear in a verse, the letters a, b, c, etc. indicate the sentence being referenced in the verse. Thus, John 11:38a means that the quotation comes from John's Gospel, chapter 11, verse 38, sentence 1.

Introduction

Rosary Primer

How to Pray the Rosary

The Mysteries

This Book

Introduction

Rosary Primer

A primer is a book that provides an introduction to a topic. This book serves as an introduction to the devotional practice known as the Rosary. The word *rosary* comes from a Sanskrit word meaning *garden of flowers* or *necklace of beads*. The word *bead* comes from an Anglo-Saxon word meaning *prayer*. Thus, the rosary is a garden of prayer or a necklace of prayer. Like any garden, to grow hearty and strong sun, rain, and fertilizer are needed. The materials in this book serve as the primer, the sun-rain-fertilizer meditation, for the garden of prayer, the rosary. A necklace wraps around the person wearing it; the rosary wraps prayer around the person using it. Hopefully, the pray-er will return to the rosary again and again to foster the growth of many flowers in his or her life and to be wrapped in prayer again and again.

The *Catechism of the Catholic Church* refers to the rosary as Marian prayer and calls it "an 'epitome of the whole gospel.'"[1] This is true because, as we will see, the four sets of mysteries are grounded in the Christian Bible (New Testament), especially the gospels, and the major events concerning the life of Jesus narrated therein. The *Catechism* also reminds us that the rosary developed "as a popular substitute for the Liturgy of the Hours" in the West.[2] When medieval people stopped coming to their local abbeys or

---

1. *Catechism*, par. 971.
2. Ibid., par. 2678.

INTRODUCTION

churches to join in morning prayer or evening prayer with the monks and clergy, they adopted a form a prayer that they could use outside the abbey or church at anytime they chose to pray. As a type of Christian prayer, the rosary invites the pray-er "above all to mediate on the mysteries of Christ."[3] Those mysteries, that is, twenty incidents from the life of Jesus that have particular spiritual significance, are worthy of reflection.

How to Pray the Rosary

It is easy to pray the rosary. However, first, a person needs to acquire a rosary, a circular string of beads organized into five sets of ten separated by a single bead between decades with a cross and five beads attached to the circle of fifty-four beads. We begin praying the rosary while touching the cross and making the sign of the cross.

> **Sign of the Cross**: With the right hand the pray-er touches the cross on the rosary to his or her forehead, saying, "In the name of the Father." Then, he or she touches the breast, saying, "and of the Son." Then, he or she touches the left shoulder and then the right, saying, "and of the Holy Spirit. Amen."

Orthodox Christians touch the right shoulder first, then the left one, while praying the same words. Thus, the prayer names the Trinity: "In the name of the Father, and of the Son, and of the Holy Spirit. Amen."

Following the Sign of the Cross, the pray-er recites the Apostles' Creed:

> **Apostles' Creed**: I believe in God, the Father almighty, Creator of heaven and earth, and in Jesus Christ, his only Son, our Lord, who was conceived by the Holy Spirit, born of the Virgin Mary, suffered under Pontius Pilate, was crucified, died, and was buried; he descended into hell; on the third day he rose again from the dead; he

---

3. Ibid., par. 2708.

Introduction

ascended into heaven, and is seated at the right hand of God the Father almighty; from there he will come to judge the living and the dead. I believe in the Holy Spirit, the holy catholic Church, the communion of saints, the forgiveness of sins, the resurrection of the body, and life everlasting. Amen.[4]

Then, going to the first large bead after the cross, he or she says the Our Father (Lord's Prayer):

Lord's Prayer: Our Father, who art in heaven, hallowed be thy name; thy kingdom come, thy will be done on earth as it is in heaven. Give us this day our daily bread, and forgive us our trespasses, as we forgive those who trespass against us; and lead us not into temptation, but deliver us from evil. Amen.[5]

Another version of the Lord's Prayer commonly prayed by Christians adds, "For thine is the kingdom, and the power, and the glory, forever and ever" before the Amen. Or "For the kingdom, the power, and the glory are yours now and forever."[6]

In the Christian Bible (New Testament), the Lord's Prayer is found in Matthew's Gospel (6:9–13) and in Luke's Gospel (11:2–4). The Lukan version is shorter than the Matthean one. The version indicated above is modeled on the one found in Matthew's Gospel, but it has been adapted to liturgical praying.

The Lord's Prayer is followed by the Hail, Mary, prayed three times, one on each of the three small beads:

Hail, Mary: Hail, Mary, full of grace! The Lord is with you; blessed are you among women, and blessed is the fruit of your womb, Jesus. Holy Mary, Mother of God, pray for us sinners, now and at the hour of our death. Amen.[7]

---

4. *Roman Missal*, "Order of Mass," par. 19.
5. Ibid., par. 124.
6. Ibid., par. 125.
7. *Catholic Source Book*, 3.

Introduction

The first sentence of the Hail, Mary, comes from Luke's Gospel (1:28), representing the archangel Gabriel's greetings to the Virgin of Nazareth. The second sentence, also from Luke's Gospel (1:42), is Elizabeth's greeting to Mary upon her arrival at Elizabeth's home. The third or last sentence, declares Mary to be the Mother of God, a statement of the Council of Ephesus in 431 CE. It also asks the Virgin to pray for us to God, just as we would ask any other person to remember us in prayer to the Holy One, today, tomorrow, and, especially, when we are preparing for death. Thus, the rosary is not a prayer to Mary, but a prayer asking the Blessed Virgin to intercede for the pray-er.

The Hail, Mary, became popular in the eleventh century. The name Jesus was added to the prayer sometime in the thirteenth century. While there were a number of versions of the prayer by the fourteenth century, the version presented above became standard by the sixteenth century.

After praying the Hail, Mary, three times, the rosary pray-er says the Glory Be:

> **Glory Be**: Glory to the Father, and to the Son, and to the Holy Spirit: as it was in the beginning, is now, and will be forever. Amen.[8]

An older version of the Glory Be is this: "Glory be to the Father, and to the Son, and to the Holy Spirit. As it was in the beginning, is now, and ever shall be, world without end. Amen."[9]

Known as a doxology, from the Greek word *doxa*, meaning *glory*, this prayer praises the Trinity—the Father, the Son, and the Holy Spirit—as existing from the beginning of time to today and for eternity. It is attributed to St. Basil the Great, a fourth-century hermit-monk, and St. Telesphorus, a second-century pope.

On the next large bead of the rosary, the first mystery is announced (for example, The Annunciation), after which one reads one of the four optional biblical verses and the reflection following it from the appropriate section of this book. When finished, the

---

8. Ibid.
9. *Scriptural Rosary*, 19.

INTRODUCTION

pray-er says the Our Father one time and the Hail, Mary, ten times, counting them on the first set of ten small beads, while mediating upon an application of the reflection that was read from this book. One may linger on each Hail, Mary, as he or she focuses attention on how the mystery being prayed is lived by the pray-er. At this point, one may want to pause and write a few reflective thoughts in his or her journal. At the end of the decade, the Glory Be is prayed. On the next large bead one announces the next mystery and proceeds through each successive decade as indicated above. After praying all five mysteries, say the Hail, Holy Queen, prayer:

> **Hail, Holy Queen**: Hail, Holy Queen, Mother of mercy, our life, our sweetness, and our hope. To you we cry, the children of Eve; to you we send up our sighs, mourning and weeping in this land of exile. Turn, then, most gracious advocate, your eyes of mercy toward us; lead us home at last, and show unto us the blessed fruit of your womb, Jesus: O clement, O loving, O sweet Virgin Mary.[10]

An older version of the Hail, Holy Queen, prayer states: "Hail, Holy Queen, Mother of Mercy, our life, our sweetness, and our hope. To you we cry, poor banished children of Eve; to you we send up our sighs, mourning and weeping in this valley of tears. Turn, then, most gracious advocate, your eyes of mercy toward us; and after this our exile, show us the blessed fruit of your womb, Jesus. O clement, O loving, O sweet Virgin Mary. (V/.) Pray for us, O holy Mother of God. (R/.) That we may be made worthy of the promises of Christ."[11]

After praying the Hail, Holy Queen, the pray-er traces the sign of the cross over himself or herself as done at the beginning and says the Sign of the Cross prayer to conclude the rosary.

There is also an optional prayer, known as the Fatima Invocation, which can be recited in between mysteries—that is, between the Glory Be that concludes one mystery and the announcement of the next mystery with its following Our Father: "O my Jesus,

---

10. *Catholic Source Book*, 17.

11. *Scriptural Rosary*, 80.

Introduction

forgive us our sins. Save us from the fires of hell, and bring all souls to heaven, especially those who most need your mercy."[12] The invocation was recommended by Mary when she appeared to the children at Fatima, Portugal, in 1917.

Counting prayers on beads is an ancient form of prayer. It is used by Christians in a variety of forms, by Muslims, and by the people of India. The use of the rosary by Christians goes back to the twelfth century and is traditionally associated with St. Dominic. On October 7, the church celebrates the Memorial of Our Lady of the Rosary, whose origin is traced to the sixteenth century.

The Mysteries

There are four sets of five mysteries each. Traditionally, the Joyful Mysteries—The Annunciation, The Visitation, The Nativity, The Presentation, and The Finding of Jesus in the Temple—are prayed on Monday and Saturday; the Luminous Mysteries—Baptism in the Jordan, The Wedding at Cana, Proclamation of the Kingdom of God, The Transfiguration, and the Institution of the Eucharist—on Thursday; the Sorrowful Mysteries—The Agony in the Garden,

---

12. *Catholic Source Book*, 16.

Introduction

The Scourging at the Pillar, The Crowning with Thorns, The Carrying of the Cross, and The Crucifixion—on Tuesday and Friday; and the Glorious Mysteries—The Resurrection, The Ascension, The Descent of the Holy Spirit Upon the Apostles, The Assumption, and The Coronation of Mary—on Sunday and Wednesday.

However, when using these reflections, pray-ers may choose to say only one decade a day from a mystery, meditate deeply upon its application in his or her life, and then spend ample time recording one's thoughts in a journal.

This Book

This book consists of eighty entries. Each entry contains the title of one of the twenty mysteries of the rosary. Following the title there is a Celebrated notation which indicates when the mystery appears on the yearly liturgical calendar. This is followed by four options from which the pray-er chooses one.

Since all but two of the mysteries are found in the Christian Bible (New Testament), each option begins with a Scripture verse or several verses which illustrate the mystery under consideration. When there is mention of the same event in all four gospels, the appropriate verse (or verses) from each gospel is presented. For example, The Baptism of Jesus in the Jordan in the Luminous Mysteries contains four options, each of which is based on one of the four gospels.

Following the Scripture selection is a short reflection. The reflection provides background to understanding the biblical text, an application for life in the twenty-first century, and a suggested focus for the reader in making a personal application of the reflection as he or she mediates on and prays the specific decade of the rosary. Each guided reflection leads the pray-er down a unique path and is intended to be returned to repeatedly in order to gain deeper insight into the mystery being prayed.

I have chosen to present four options for each individual mystery. In subsequent prayings of the rosary, the pray-er may choose another optional biblical text and reflection to guide his or her

Introduction

meditation. Furthermore, in biblical literature, the number four (4) represents the created order, that is, the earth. Since the earth is where we live, and since there are four gospels, four optional reflections, each with its own biblical verse, enable us to explore the depth of the mystery. All entries—except for The Assumption and The Coronation of Mary—are based on Christian Bible (New Testament) texts that highlight each mystery or some aspect of the mystery under consideration. For the two exceptions, which are not mentioned in the Bible, I present biblical texts that underlie the mystery being explored.

Rosary pray-ers need biblical material to reflect upon while navigating a mystery with its set of five illustrative mysteries. In-depth meditation requires plenty of quiet time. First, a person clears his or her mind of all the things that seem to crowd in there. Then, slowly and devoutly, he or she begins to pray. Prayer cannot be forced or controlled; it can only be nudged through an openness on the part of the pray-er. One must be careful not to get caught up in saying prayers but not actually praying! While resting and at peace with God, the pray-er may turn to a mystery in this book, choose an option, read the words of the Scripture passage, read the reflection following it, and say the required Hail, Mary, ten times. However, the process is the means to listen deeply and intently to what God is praying in the person. As one listens and responds to God, prayer oozes everywhere. When that conversation is finished, one may wish to continue to reflect upon what was heard or re-read the Scripture and reflection in this book before writing his or her thoughts in a journal. A spiral-bound notebook or some other type of diary can be used. Not only does a person record his or her thoughts, but he or she can refer to them time after time. In other words, there is a big difference between praying and saying prayers.

While the chronological order of the gospels is Mark (written around 70 CE), Matthew (written around 80 CE), Luke (written around 90 CE), and John (written around 100 CE), I've chosen to follow the biblical book order found in the Christian Bible (New Testament): Matthew, Mark, Luke, John, Acts, Letters of Paul, etc.

Introduction

For the benefit of the reader, as noted above, I have included a Celebrated indicator for each mystery. The Celebrated indicator identifies when each specific mystery is marked on the liturgical calendar of the Roman Catholic Church. This notation is designed to help the reader locate the solemnity, feast, or memorial within the broader picture of the whole church in terms of Scripture, reflection, and celebration of each of the twenty mysteries of the rosary.

It is my hope that this book will further deepen the prayer, reflection, and mediation of those who use it while praying the mysteries of the rosary.

Mark G. Boyer
Our Lady of the Rosary
October 7, 2017

1

Joyful Mysteries

The Annunciation

The Visitation

The Nativity

The Presentation

The Finding of Jesus in the Temple

The Annunciation

Celebrated: March 25, The Annunciation of the Lord

Option 1

Scripture: ". . . An angel of the Lord appeared to [Joseph] in a dream and said, 'Joseph, son of David, do not be afraid to take Mary as your wife, for the child conceived in her is from the Holy Spirit.'" (Matt 1:20–21)

Reflection: The author of Matthew's Gospel tells the story of the annunciation differently than the author of Luke's Gospel. In Luke, the angel Gabriel appears to Mary. In Matthew, the angel of the Lord—an Old Testament code for God—speaks to Joseph in a dream and announces that his fiancée, Mary, has conceived through the Holy Spirit and will give birth to a child Joseph will name Jesus.

The Joseph of Matthew's Gospel resembles Joseph, son of Jacob, in the Hebrew Bible (Old Testament). He is a dreamer; he experiences God in his dreams. Just like Joseph, son of Jacob, has the ability to interpret dreams—both his own and those of a pharaoh—so does Joseph, fiancée of Mary, interpret the dreams God sends to him.

Because Matthew's Gospel features Joseph—unlike Luke's Gospel which features Mary—the Matthean form of the annunciation may appeal more to men. Married men have a vision of what they want their family to be and how they hope to provide for family needs. God may speak to men through their goals and expectations, which may often mean thinking outside of the box or looking at alternative plans. Joseph was getting ready to break the engagement with Mary when he discovers her pregnancy. Through his dream, God enlarged his vision of what the Holy One was planning for the world.

For men today, their vision might have to be widened to include a move from one city to another in order to keep a good job. It may entail living in one city and driving to work in another at some distance away. As any parent can attest, a wife and children move back the boundaries of one's perspective radically. And once a family is begun, the days of sitting on the couch watching football may be over!

As you pray this joyful mystery, reflect on some of the recent dreams that you have received from God. And do not be afraid of the announcement that God delivers to you through them.

Option 2

Scripture: [Gabriel announced to Mary,] "... [Y]ou will conceive in your womb and bear a son, and you will name him Jesus." (Luke 1:31)

Reflection: Every major event culminates in an announcement of some kind. Ancient kings of long-forgotten cities recorded the announcement of the defeat of their enemies on clay tablets, papyrus scrolls, and parchment sheets. Sometimes they erected a stele or an arch to serve as a perpetual announcement concerning the event. Egyptian pharaohs kept a scribe at hand at all times just in case they might make an announcement of desert-shaking proportions.

The author of Luke's Gospel thinks that the imminent birth of Jesus deserves a similar announcement. The angel Gabriel—meaning *God's strength*—announces to Mary that the Holy Spirit will come upon her and God's power will overshadow her and she will give birth to a Son of the Most High God, a Spirit-child, who will be named Jesus.

The practice of ancient kings and pharaohs and gospel writers continues today. A graduation from high school and college is usually announced through the mail with an invitation. The imminent union of a man and woman is accounted as an engagement in the Sunday newspaper. It will reappear there later as a wedding announcement. Family and friends of the bride and groom will receive wedding announcements. The announcement of a baby shower precedes the annunciation of the baby's birth. And most newspapers contain an obituary section announcing the deaths of members of the community.

Announcements come into our lives from God, too, all the time. While they may not be accompanied by an angel, God announces new ideas to us through our reading. Watch a movie and God might announce something important through one of the characters. Listen intently to a spouse or a friend and hear God give the solution to a problem. When one's conscience dictates what one knows to be the right thing to do, when one speaks the truth, when one accepts full responsibility for one's action, he or she can be assured that he or she is hearing announcements from God.

As you pray this joyful mystery, reflect on some of the recent announcements that you have received from God. And be joyful that God continues to announce good news to you.

Option 3

Scripture: ". . . [T]he angel said to [the shepherds], 'Do not be afraid; for see—I am bringing you good news of great joy for all

JOYFUL MYSTERIES

the people: to you is born this day in the city of David a Savior, who is the Messiah, the Lord.'" (Luke 2:10–11)

Reflection: Besides the annunciation of the angel of the Lord to Joseph and the archangel Gabriel to Mary, there is also the annunciation of "an angel of the Lord" in Luke's Gospel. The angel appears to the poor shepherds keeping watch over their flocks of sheep during the night. They are startled by the appearance of the angel's light—God's glory—in the darkness of the night. However, the angel displays the very message that the angel is about to deliver, namely, that the light of Jesus' birth has shattered the darkness of the world.

Indeed, this is good news of great joy. Any time good news of great joy floods our lives light scatters darkness. It may be the good news of the birth of a healthy child that drives away the darkness of doubt. It may be the good news of a new job that removes the night of fear.

A student may welcome the good news of a passing grade that removes the blackness of possible failure of a course. When the good news of peace arrives, be assured that the shadows of war are illuminated.

There is no need to fear because God is in the announcement. It's no accident that God sends an angel to announce good news to shepherds out in the fields. In Luke's Gospel, the shepherds represent the poor for whom Jesus has a special concern. Throughout both the gospel and throughout the second volume by the same author, the Acts of the Apostles, the poor are the locus of care and concern. In order to emphasize this point, Luke introduces the theme of the importance of the poor with the announcement of the angel to the shepherds and their ensuing pilgrimage to visit the baby Jesus. In fact the shepherds themselves become vehicles of the good news as they announce everywhere and to everyone that Jesus is the Messiah, the Anointed One of God.

As you pray this joyful mystery, reflect on some good news that someone has brought to you. That person may be an angel—God in disguise—sharing with you some great joy for you and all those around you.

Option 4

Scripture: [Jesus said,] "See, I am coming soon; my reward is with me, to repay according to everyone's work. I am the Alpha and the Omega, the first and the last, the beginning and the end." (Rev 22:12–13)

Reflection: The Book of Revelation contains several announcements, some made by its author, John of Patmos, and some by Jesus himself. Towards the end of the book, Jesus declares that he is coming soon. During Advent the church focuses on his coming in three ways.

First, there is a focus on his coming in history—his birth. Second, people prepare for his coming every day in their lives. And third, they look forward to his return at the end of time. Jesus' announcement in the Book of Revelation that he is "coming soon" reminds all of the last two of the three foci of Advent. But Advent is meant to be a miniature of a theme that should be woven throughout daily life.

So, as you pray this joyful mystery, you might reflect on all the ways that Jesus comes daily. It may be in the person of a member of your family who greets you in the morning before he or she leaves for work or school and in the evening after returning home from the same. It may be that Jesus comes in a person you see in the grocery, hardware, or jewelry store. A quiet moment standing at the kitchen sink and getting lost in what you are doing—cleaning, preparing food, gazing out the window—may be the occasion for Jesus to visit. If you serve on a committee or participate in some parish ministry, Jesus may appear in the other members of your group or in those you serve.

You may choose to pray this joyful mystery and reflect upon Jesus' promise to return at the end of time. Every time we celebrate Eucharist, the minister reminds us after we recite the Lord's Prayer that we are awaiting the blessed hope, the coming of our Savior, Jesus Christ. No one knows when that will occur; some have said that it takes place as soon as we die. In the gospels Jesus makes it clear that only God knows when he will return.

Joyful Mysteries

Whatever your focus on this joyful mystery is remember that Jesus is the Alpha and the Omega, the first and last letters of the Greek alphabet. This means that he encompasses everything from the beginning to the end.

The Visitation

Celebrated: May 31, The Visitation of the Blessed Virgin Mary

Option 1

Scripture: "... Mary set out and went with haste to a Judean town in the hill country, where she entered the house of Zechariah and greeted Elizabeth." (Luke 1:39–40)

Reflection: If we visit an ill friend in the hospital, we think of ourselves as the visitor. Likewise, if we visit a relative in a nursing home, we consider ourselves to be the visitor. Those involved in hospice care know that they visit and care for those who are near death.

In Luke's unique story of Mary visiting Elizabeth, we at first conclude that Mary is the visitor and Elizabeth is the visited. And on the surface level, that is true. Mary has journeyed to Zechariah's and Elizabeth's home to see them. But Mary has already been visited by God in the person of Gabriel. So, as she proceeds to visit Elizabeth, she discovers that God has not only already visited Elizabeth, but that Elizabeth serves the role of visitor also. This means that she receives Mary as the mother of the Lord and she shares the good that has been entrusted to her, namely, that she has been filled with the Holy Spirit, bears the Lord's forerunner—John the Baptist—in her own womb, and that there are plenty of God's blessings to go around. In other words, the visitor, Mary, becomes the visited, and the visited, Elizabeth, becomes the visitor.

We can measure our self-worth by how well we visit others. Mary and Elizabeth lived in a culture that measured hospitality in terms of what was received from others. Instead of approaching a friend in the hospital with the preconceived idea that you are the visitor and he or she is the visited, try making your visit one in which you are open to receive from the ill person. Likewise, when visiting a relative in a nursing home, focus on what you receive from the elderly or handicapped. Even though you may make the trip, those who have suffered, those who have lived, those who have loved have many gifts to offer their visitors.

For example, by listening to the words of the elderly, you might discover a solution to your problem. By listening to the sick, you might discover the power of suffering. We never know when our visit to another may turn out to be a visit of the other to us. God is always the first to visit us during prayer when we may actually think we are visiting God!

As you pray this joyful mystery, reflect on some of the recent visitations that you have received from others and God when you thought you were doing the visiting. Be joyful that God continues to visit you.

Option 2

Scripture: "When Elizabeth heard Mary's greeting, the child leaped in her womb. And Elizabeth was filled with the Holy Spirit and exclaimed with a loud cry, 'Blessed are you among women, and blessed is the fruit of your womb.'" (Luke 1:41–42)

Reflection: As soon as Mary greets Elizabeth, Elizabeth is visited by the Holy Spirit. The author of Luke's Gospel here utilizes a theme unique to his two-volume work. The Holy Spirit guides everyone in the gospel, and the Holy Spirit guides everyone in the Acts of the Apostles. In other words, God accomplishes the divine mission through the outpouring of the Holy Spirit.

The visitation of the Holy Spirit begins earlier in Luke's Gospel when Gabriel tells Mary that the Holy Spirit will come upon her, and the power of the Most High will overshadow her. The child to whom she will give birth will be a Spirit-boy. He is filled with the Holy Spirit from the moment of his conception; he is led by the Holy Spirit throughout his ministry; he returns the Holy Spirit to his Father before he dies. Then, he sees to it that God pours out the Holy Spirit in two Pentecosts—Jewish and Gentile—in the Acts of the Apostles.

While we don't want to anticipate the Glorious Mystery of the Descent of the Holy Spirit Upon the Apostles, here we want to focus on how the Holy Spirit visits us. Through deep and intense prayer, we may experience a connection to God that results in powerful peace; that's an experience of the visitation of the Holy Spirit. After mulling over and over a problem and looking at it from many possible perspectives, we experience the guidance of the Holy Spirit as we know exactly what we need to do. An insight into the truth of a situation which arrives through reading or conversation is often a visitation of the Holy Spirit. The communion in love shared between husband and wife is the Holy Spirit visiting them.

Whenever the Holy Spirit visits, those who recognize the Divine Presence usually discover themselves bursting out in joy. Elizabeth pronounces two beatitudes: One declares Mary blessed among women, and the other declares blessed the fruit of her womb, her child.

As you pray this joyful mystery, reflect on some of the recent visitations that you have received from the Holy Spirit. Be joyful that the Holy Spirit inspires you.

Option 3

Scripture: [Elizabeth said to Mary,] ". . . As soon as I heard the sound of your greeting, the child in my womb leaped for joy. And blessed is she who believed that there would be a fulfillment of what was spoken to her by the Lord." (Luke 1:44–45)

Reflection: The Joyful Mystery of the annunciation includes Elizabeth's annunciation that the child in her womb—John the Baptist—leaped for joy when she heard Mary's initial greeting upon entering Zechariah's home. While Elizabeth is referring specifically to her pregnancy, we might expand our reflections to any greeting that makes us leap for joy.

For example, is there not a special feeling deep down inside us when we get some good news? It might be the announcement of something for which we have longed and hoped, such as a job promotion, a book that has sold well, a family member's visit, or someone's cure from cancer. It may be a surprise announcement, like an invitation to a wedding in the mail, an unexpected check, a bouquet of flowers, or a birthday card. The announcement may be from those who appear regularly in our lives, like a child who comes home with a great report card, a spouse who has gotten a raise, or a college friend who calls with the excitement of his or her first job. Something new, like a pregnancy, stirs deep down inside of us, and we know that we have been visited by God.

As sacramental people, Roman Catholics are always celebrating God's deeply stirring visitations. God visits us in baptism with new life. God arrives in confirmation with Holy Spirit. Through our celebration of Eucharist, Christ is made present. We are forgiven by God's visit in Penance, and healed by God's touch in Anointing of the Sick. In the sacrament of Matrimony, God comes

Joyful Mysteries

to dwell in the person of the other. And in Holy Orders, those who lead and guide us assure us of God's presence.

As Elizabeth makes clear to Mary in Elizabeth's beatitude, something from God has been fulfilled. Part of God's mission is accomplished. And human beings are the vehicles for that!

As you pray this joyful mystery, reflect on some of the recent ways that God has visited you. As you do so, be aware that God is fulfilling part of the Holy One's mission through your faith in the Divine Word.

Option 4

Scripture: "When the angels had left them and gone into heaven, the shepherds said to one another, 'Let us go now to Bethlehem and see this thing that has taken place, which the Lord has made to known to us.'" (Luke 2:15)

Reflection: Once the angels of the Lord visit the shepherds keeping watch during the night over their flocks in the field, they decide to go see for themselves the child wrapped in bands of cloth and lying in a manger. In other words, after receiving God's visitation and being given a sign, the poor shepherds conclude that it would be a good idea to check it out. And so they do.

Often times, God's visitations to us require us to do something. God doesn't just visit us, pat us on the back, and then leave. There is always a mission upon which we are sent; we are given a task, some job, something for which we must be responsible.

For example, God visits parents through the person of their doctor with the good news that they are going to have a child. They are now responsible for a new life. Not only will they have to bring that new life to birth, but they have to plan on nurturing that life for the next eighteen to twenty years or more.

God may visit you with the bad news of cancer. Such an announcement through your doctor can be the occasion for a pity party. Or it can be an opportunity to test a new drug, help support other patients who are present for your chemotherapy treatments, or a witness to the power of uniting your suffering to that of Christ.

If you want to be visited by God, try volunteering time in your local soup kitchen or center that helps the poor. The Holy One has a special fondness for the poor—as seen throughout the Hebrew Bible (Old Testament) and the Christian Bible (New Testament). Giving away some time to serve others will stir up a mission inside you which may take the shape of proclaiming the dignity of all people, helping to eradicate poverty in your area, or raising funds to support the shelter where you work.

The shepherds decide to go see what God has told them. They fulfill their mission by finding the Christ child and, then, telling all they have seen to whomever will listen to them.

As you pray this joyful mystery, reflect on some of your recent visitations and the missions that have been attached to them. Be joyful for what God has made known to you.

The Nativity

Celebrated: December 25, The Nativity of the Lord [Christmas]

Joyful Mysteries

Option 1

Scripture: "... [Joseph] took [Mary] as his wife, but had no marital relations with her until she had borne a son; and he named him Jesus." (Matt 1:24b–25)

Reflection: There are many points of view from which to describe the affects a birth has on other people. A doctor delivering a child would narrate the story from a birthing procedure point of view and tell how it followed usual medical protocol or taxed the doctor's knowledge of medicine. The father of the child would tell it from the perspective of coaching the mother, and how much effort he had to put forth to keep her focused on the task at hand. The mother's point of view would probably begin with the end of her nine-month pregnancy and work backward to the time of conception. If the child could talk, he or she would explain what it is like to be evicted from a warm home after only nine months of residency, forced through a canal towards bright lights, and promptly have every orifice suctioned before being washed and wrapped in a blanket.

The author of Matthew's Gospel tells of Jesus' nativity from the point of view of how his birth will affect other people. Matthew is concerned with Jesus' birth from a Gentile perspective, featuring a story about magi arriving at Joseph's and Mary's house with funerary gifts of gold, frankincense, and myrrh for the child. According to Matthew's Gospel, Jesus came to gather both Jews and Gentiles into God's reign above the heavens before he died.

Your birth has affected a lot of people. Your parents might tell your nativity story from the point of view of the great changes you made in their lives. Your grandparents would tell the story from the perspective of a new grandchild and all they wanted to do for you. How would your pre-school and kindergarten teachers tell the affect you had on their lives? What point of view would your elementary principal choose? How about your high school classmates? What affect have you had on your friends? We often make it through a lifetime and never take time to think about all the people whose lives we have touched and affected.

As you reflect on this joyous mystery of the nativity of Jesus and how his birth affected his world, examine your birth from the point of view of the ways you have affected the people who inhabit your world.

Option 2

Scripture: "[Mary] gave birth to her firstborn son and wrapped him in bands of cloth, and laid him in a manger, because there was no place for them in the inn." (Luke 2:7)

Reflection: The Lukan account of the Nativity differs considerably from its Matthean counterpart. Luke uses his story to introduce a theme that he will exploit throughout his gospel and his second volume, the Acts of the Apostles. The particular theme introduced here is that Jesus, who eats meals with the outcasts, is also food.

After narrating how Joseph and Mary respond to Emperor Augustus's decree concerning registration, Luke explains how the couple left Nazareth in Galilee and traveled to Bethlehem. After Mary gives birth to her child, Jesus, she lays him in a manger, a feeding trough for animals. Thus, Jesus is portrayed as food for one's journey of faith.

This theme is woven through Luke's Gospel in his portrayal of Jesus eating meals and giving himself as food. For example, Peter abandons a great catch of fish in order to follow Jesus, the true food. Jesus instructs his disciples that the poor, the maimed, the lame, and the blind should be invited to the banquet. And, of course, Jesus gives himself as food and drink before he dies.

Thus, it is no accident that the Nativity of the Lord, Christmas, is marked by most families with food. The table is spread with turkey, goose, or ham; side dishes of sweet potatoes, green bean casserole, dressing, and salad surround the main course. And as all gather and sit around the table, the family members do more than just fill their plates and eat of the feast. Each person is food for every other person around the table. When the bowl of mashed potatoes is passed, so is Uncle Henry, Aunt Jane, Grandfather John, and Grandmother Mary shared.

A nativity of any kind sparks a desire in people to gather together and eat a meal. Even a newborn child, who is not ready for solid food, is brought to the table. Through food, that child is initiated into a family.

As you pray this joyful mystery, reflect upon all the meal-sharing you do. Think about what birthing takes place as you and your family members sit down and eat a meal together and how each is food for all others.

Option 3

Scripture: "In the beginning was the Word, and the Word was with God, and the Word was God. And the Word became flesh and lived among us...." (John 1:1, 14)

Reflection: The author of John's Gospel begins his work with a reflection on the origins of God's Word which echoes the opening lines of the Book of Genesis. John understands God's Word, Jesus, to have existed always; there was never a time when he was not. However, at a certain point in history God spoke, and the Word became flesh. God became incarnate, embodied, in a human being who left footprints on the earth. The nativity in John's Gospel is a revelation of God's glory that has always existed. The Holy One, who cannot be seen, is now seen in the face of the Father's only Son, Jesus Christ.

In the past, God revealed the Divine Presence in the act of creation, especially making man and woman in the image of the Holy One. God was also revealed in the rainbow to Noah, in fire to Abraham, Moses, and Isaiah, in dreams to Joseph and Daniel, and even as a tiny whispering sound to Elijah. But in the person of Jesus Christ, the Mighty One took the form of a human being and was born in time and walked among us. That's why we call it incarnation, becoming flesh.

While we may not think about it, in some degree we, too, speak words and they become flesh. For example, we begin to plan a trip in January for July. Gradually, we gather what we need: a passport, a suitcase, new clothes. And as we drive or fly or float to our destination, we make the trip flesh. A couple speaks vows about freedom to marry, fidelity, and openness to children, and, through their words, they make present a marriage that has not before existed. A writer takes letters and creates words, and from the words he or she composes sentences which may become a book. On the day a book is published, any writer will tell you that it is like giving birth.

If we just sit back and contemplate, we'll discover that every day things are coming to be because we speak words. Nativities are happening all around us; none of course can rival the Incarnation.

As you pray this joyful mystery, reflect upon all the words you speak. Think about what comes to be because of the words you speak, how they live among us, and how they reveal God's glory.

Option 4

Scripture: "[The woman] was pregnant and was crying out in birth pangs, in the agony of giving birth. And she gave birth to a son, a male child, who is to rule all the nations with a rod of iron." (Rev 12:2, 5)

Reflection: In the Book of Revelation, John of Patmos writes about the pregnant woman who gives birth to a son while being pursued by a red dragon. Because he never names her, she could be Eve, Israel, or Mary. As Eve, the woman's enemy is the serpent; she gives birth to Cain, who kills his brother, Abel, and Seth. As Israel, she gives birth to a covenant with God. As Mary, she gives birth to Jesus. She may even represent all three simultaneously.

The focus of her birthing is on something new. Cain, Abel, and Seth are the first children of Adam and Eve; they are the first children ever to be born. Israel's covenant with God is the first to have been initiated by God with a chosen band of nomads. And Jesus was the firstborn son of Mary.

A nativity is the means for God to do something new. Every person ever born is a new creation; that's why no two of us are ever alike. And with the person's cooperation, God can birth something new. Sometimes people call it God's plan or one's destiny. The name for it matters little; the Holy One is doing something new in the life of every birth.

A nativity may herald a concert pianist, a rocket scientist, a mathematician, an accountant, a racer, a gymnast, an author, a truck driver, a president, etc. And those and many other human possibilities—both those we can imagine and those we cannot yet even begin to imagine—are occasions for God to make something new in the world. God is always renewing the world through the birth of something or someone new.

Sometimes it takes years for the new to be born. Sometimes it occurs within a few minutes. Be assured that God is always seeing to it that something new is taking place. In our day and through his birth, the male Christ child rules the world with the rod of his cross, and that, indeed, is something new.

As you reflect on this mystery, name what God has done new in the world through you. Think about what newness takes place through you, and be joyful that God keeps working in your life.

The Presentation

Celebrated: February 2, The Presentation of the Lord

Option 1

Scripture: "After eight days had passed, it was time to circumcise the child; and he was called Jesus, the name given by the angel before he was conceived in the womb." (Luke 2:21)

Reflection: In the world of the first century, circumcision was practiced by the Jews and not by the Gentiles. For the Jews circumcision represented incorporation into the covenant that God had established with Abraham. That covenant stipulated that the LORD would be Abraham's God, and Abraham and his descendants would be the Holy One's chosen people. Circumcision was done on the eighth day because eight represents completion—as in a musical octave today.

The author of Luke's Gospel wants his readers to understand that Jesus is Jewish; he has been incorporated into the Abrahamic covenant. Out of the old covenant, which included the shedding of blood, he will establish a new one in his blood. Luke's unique account of Jesus' circumcision foreshadows his death on the cross. Of the Synoptic Gospels (Matthew, Mark, Luke), only Luke portrays Jesus declaring at the Last Supper that the cup is the new covenant that will be established in his blood. In other words, out of the old Israel Luke sees the birth of a new Israel that incorporates all people—Jews and Gentiles. Thus, Jesus, whose name means *the Lord saves* or *Yahweh helps*, is presented as the Savior of the world.

While circumcision is routinely practiced in the United States of America, such is not the case throughout the world. Some peoples consider it mutilation. Others, such as Jews, still practice it as a sign of entry into the covenant God established with Abraham and renewed with Moses. So, instead of focusing on the physical act of circumcision, we might spend time with what the Bible often calls the circumcision of one's heart.

We can present to God a circumcised heart, one that has removed everything that gets in the way of our relationship with the Holy One. If materialism, an excessive desire for things and money, is what blocks us from God, then we need to circumcise it. If individualism, an extravagant focus on self, blockades us from

Joyful Mysteries

the Most High, then we need to circumcise it. Addictions—such as alcohol, smoking, drugs, cell phones—can be barriers in our path to God; they need to be circumcised from our lives, our hearts. In any case, some blood will be shed.

As you pray this mystery, focus on your heart and what needs to be circumcised from it. Be joyful that God has chosen you to participate in the new covenant established in the blood of his Son.

Option 2

Scripture: "When the time came for [Joseph and Mary's] purification according to the law of Moses, they brought [Jesus] up to Jerusalem to present him to the Lord...." (Luke 2:22)

Reflection: An introduction of one person to another can more accurately be called a presentation. One person says to another, "John, may I present to you Mary." And the other responds, 'I am pleased to meet you, Mary." The French usually respond with "*Enchante*," meaning "I am enchanted, or pleased, to meet you." During an elegant ball, daughters of prominent citizens are presented to members of a country club. During the half-time of a football or basketball game, the nominees for homecoming king and queen and their escorts are presented both to former and current students in a high school.

In Luke's unique story, Jesus is presented in the Jerusalem Temple by Joseph and Mary. The Spirit-conceived child in effect is brought to his Father's house where he is presented to God. As Luke narrates the story, two elderly and wise people recognize and explain the meaning of Jesus' presentation. First, Simeon, filled with the Holy Spirit, declares that Jesus will be a light both for Jews and Gentiles. Second, Anna speaks about the redemption of Jerusalem that will be accomplished through Jesus.

Simeon and Anna represent the wisdom of the older years. There is something about age that knows—that recognizes truth— that can discern the deep-down certitude of things and share it with others. Most of the time we associate wisdom with grandparents, who instruct their grandchildren in truths that parents cannot seem to communicate. In our culture, mentors serve the same purpose; they take young men and women and explore with them the issues that really matter to them: relationships, love, life, spirituality, sex, and death. Teachers are also dispensers of wisdom; there are instructors who give more than course materials. They inspire learning that lasts a lifetime instead of memorizing what is quickly forgotten.

As Simeon and Ann make clear, God can be recognized in countless presentations if we but open our eyes and hearts. As you pray this mystery, reflect upon all the truth and joy that has come to you from God through others who have been presented to you.

Option 3

Scripture: "Long ago God spoke to our ancestors in many and various ways by the prophets, but in these last days he has spoken to us by a Son . . . . He is the reflection of God's glory and the exact imprint of God's very being . . . ." (Heb 1:1–3)

Reflection: In times past, God spoke through the prophets, states the author of the Letter to the Hebrews. Such truth is enshrined in the Profession of Faith, recited on Sundays and Holy Days. After declaring that they believe in the Holy Spirit, catholics state that God has spoken through the prophets. God, in the person of the Holy Spirit, has repeatedly called people to repentance or provided hope through the words of those who speak in the Holy One's name.

However, the Mighty One even surpassed the major prophets—Isaiah, Jeremiah, and Ezekiel—by speaking in the person of Jesus Christ, God's only Son. So, if there were reason to listen to the prophets of the past, there is even more reason to listen to the Son whom God has presented to the world; he shares all that the Eternal One is and reflects the Mighty One's glory. In other words, the Son shares the Father's very essence; the Son incarnates God's word for us.

The Son's reflection of God's essence is presented to us so that we can recognize and share in it through our obedience in faith to the God of all. We get glimpses of God's glory through our own human relationships. Standing transparent—truthful, honest, authentic—before one we love enables the beloved to see through us to the One who gives meaning to all relationships. Gazing into the eyes of our beloved—spouse, friend, spiritual director—and knowing the truth of the words he or she speaks causes God's glory to shine. Enjoying some time alone with a spouse or friend while eating a meal enables us to connect to the other in a way that displays the glory of God shared by the Son.

Through our human relating, God continues to display the divine relationship of Father and Son and Holy Spirit. We cannot yet share in the fullness of the three Persons in One God, but we can glimpse the glory that our ancestors shared when they heard the Holy One's voice through the prophets and, even better, when they heard the preaching and teaching of Jesus.

As you reflect on this mystery, think about how God's glory is revealed in your life, especially in your relationships, as you hear God's word. Be joyful that your human relationships assist you with your divine relationship.

Option 4

Scripture: "... [W]hen Christ came into the world, he said ..., 'See, God, I have come to do your will, O God.' And it is by God's will that we have been sanctified through the offering of the body of Jesus Christ once for all." (Heb 10:5, 7, 10)

Reflection: According to the Letter to the Hebrews, the world we experience on earth had a parallel in heaven until the time of Jesus, who formed a bridge between the two worlds. The sacrifices offered on the altar in Jerusalem's Temple could not completely eradicate sin; only the self-offering of Christ could do that. And that self-offering is what God willed. Thus, from the perspective of Hebrews, Jesus served as the priest—the one who made the offering—and sacrifice—he who was offered. In other words, once for all Jesus offered himself to God in order to do God's will for the sanctification of all.

Christ's presentation of himself to God as a once-for-all sacrifice was the Holy One's will. And what God willed for Jesus, the Mighty One also wills for us. Our lifetime task as followers of Christ is to conform ourselves more and more to the likeness of Jesus in presenting ourselves to God as a sacrifice. We are to grow into doing God's will until we are so much like Christ that we are ready to hand over our lives to the Holy One.

Every time we celebrate the Eucharist we present ourselves to God as a sacrifice. When the gifts of bread and wine are presented, all the members of the church are presented. Just as many grains of wheat are ground to produce a single loaf of bread, so we, though many, are one body of Christ. As many grapes are squeezed to produce one cup of wine, so we, though many, are one blood of Christ. When the priest prays the Eucharistic Prayer, he offers the bread and wine—the body of Christ and us—to God as a sacrifice that sanctifies us and the whole world.

Throughout the week, we present sacrifices to God. We may fast, abstain, share financial resources with the poor, volunteer in a soup kitchen or a hospital. No matter what we do, we imitate Christ in doing God's will: We offer ourselves to God in sacrifice. Those little sacrifices lead up to, flow from, and give meaning to the eucharistic sacrifice we present every Sunday.

As you pray this joyful mystery, think about all the little sacrifices you make that confirm that you are doing God's will. Make a conscious effort to bring those to Mass on Sunday and unite them to the once-for-all offering of Christ.

Joyful Mysteries

The Finding of Jesus in the Temple

Celebrated: The Sunday within the Octave of the Nativity of the Lord [Christmas] (between December 25 and January 1), or, if there is no Sunday, December 30, The Holy Family of Jesus, Mary, and Joseph

Option 1

Scripture: [Jesus said,] "Day after day I was with you in the temple teaching, and you did not arrest me. But let the scriptures be fulfilled." (Mark 14:49)

Reflection: In Marks' Gospel, Jesus seems to have a love-hate relationship with the Jerusalem Temple. After he enters Jerusalem triumphantly, he merely looks around at the Temple. The next day he engages in some serious house cleaning by driving out both buyers and sellers. Likewise, Jesus teaches in the Temple and predicts its destruction. After he is arrested as a bandit, he reminds the crowd that he was in the Temple daily, teaching them.

The author of Mark's Gospel does not provide a boyhood finding-in-the-Temple story, like the author of Luke's Gospel does. For Mark, Jesus is found in the Temple, one of the places where God was located, only during the last few days of his life. Mark locates him there to validate his prediction that not one Temple stone would be left upon another one; by the time Mark's Gospel was finished, Jerusalem and the Temple had been destroyed by the Romans.

Mark also enables the reader to find Jesus in the Temple because it is the locus for the enactment of the proclamation of the presence of the kingdom of God. After Jesus dies, the narrator of Mark's Gospel makes clear that the curtain in the Temple is torn apart from top to bottom to signal that God has gotten out; this passage echoes the torn-apart heavens at his baptism and his ensuing proclamation of God's kingdom. God is no longer located above the heavens or in the Temple on earth; God's kingdom is now everywhere, spread throughout the universe.

Thus, in Mark's Gospel finding Jesus in the Temple is nebulous. When he is found there, he is always debating with the authorities or telling stories that put them down. The old, represented by the Temple, is giving way to the new, represented by Jesus and his proclamation of the kingdom of God.

As you pray this last joyful mystery, think about how Jesus replaces the Temple with his proclamation of God's kingdom. Then name your own temples—your old ways of prayer, service, contributions, ways of thinking, etc.—and determine if some of those need to be destroyed to make way for God's kingdom where you find Jesus in the new temple, the church, the body of Christ, etc.

Option 2

Scripture: "After three days [Joseph and Mary] found [Jesus] in the temple, sitting among the teachers, listening to them and asking them questions." (Luke 2:46)

Reflection: The only canonical story of Jesus as a boy is found in Luke's Gospel. Jesus is twelve years old. He and his parents have just been to Jerusalem for Passover, the annual celebration of Hebrew liberation from Egyptian bondage. Mary and Joseph think that their child is with others on the return trip home, but he has stayed in Jerusalem, where, after three days, they find him in the Temple. Of course, this account of Jesus being found in the Temple is meant to parallel his presentation in the Temple. The author has even crafted similar endings for both stories. Luke portrays Jesus, the Spirit-child, being presented to God in the Temple in the previous story; in this one he portrays Jesus as superior to the Temple authorities. However, his focus is on who is lost. At first glance it looks like Jesus is lost, but upon careful consideration, we begin to see that the authorities are lost in amazement at Jesus' understanding and questions.

When something is lost, we attempt to find it. So, we hunt for the lost car keys and find them in a purse, on a table, or in a pocket. Coins are always falling between the sofa cushions, rolling under the refrigerator, or disappearing into the floor vents; they are found by those who clean the house. Usually, lost tools can be found where they were last used. Because of our focus on looking for lost things, we may never consider ourselves lost and in need of being found.

And that is the key to understanding the story of Jesus being lost in the Temple. See, he is not lost; the Spirit-child is in God's house on earth where he belongs. The temple authorities are lost, and his parents are lost. None of them understands what he says to them.

We cannot find God, no matter how hard we search; God finds us. It might be in prayer, it might be in ranching, it might be in cleaning, it might be in family relationships that God finds us. We can get too distracted thinking that we are the searchers, instead of waiting to be found by God.

As you pray this mystery, reflect upon all the ways that God has found you through others. And be joyful that God seeks the lost.

Option 3

Scripture: [The angel of the Lord said to the apostles,] "'Go, stand in the temple and tell the people the whole message about this life.' When they heard this, they entered the temple at daybreak and went on with their teaching." (Acts 5:20–21)

Reflection: Because the apostles are so successful in curing the sick, the high priest and those aligned with him have the apostles arrested and put in prison. During the night, however, an angel of the Lord opens the prison doors and sets them free. The author of the Acts of the Apostles, the same person who wrote Luke's Gospel, employs the exodus theme here to indicate that God is still delivering chosen people from bondage.

The next day, when the high priest is ready to interrogate the apostles, he asks to have them brought in, but, of course, they are no longer in prison. They are found in the Temple, teaching the people. After they were found and questioned, they were flogged. And they went back to the Temple to proclaim Jesus as the Messiah.

Because the apostles are witnesses to all that Jesus taught and preached, they cannot be deterred from the Temple, where they can always find an audience who will listen to them. Furthermore, even the anger of and beating by Jewish authorities will not stop them. In fact, they rejoice that they are worthy to suffer for the sake of proclaiming Jesus' name.

While there is no longer any Temple in Jerusalem, we might widen our reflection to include all the places of our day where we might bear witness to the name of Jesus. If we hear a joke or gossip that denigrates a group of people, do we speak up for their human dignity for the sake of the name we bear? If we see someone walking out of a store with something for which he or she did not pay, do we speak up for the sake of honesty? Do we always tell the truth, even when such veracity may not make us look good, or have we become experts at avoiding responsibility for our actions?

As you pray this joyful mystery, reflect on the way that you bear witness to the name of Jesus, the Messiah. If you discover that you are not faithful to the name of Christian—follower of

Christ—that you bear, begin to correct that. If you discover that you suffer for being who you are, consider yourself worthy to sacrifice for the sake of the name.

Option 4

Scripture: ". . . Christ did not enter a sanctuary made by human hands, a mere copy of the true one, but he entered into heaven itself, now to appear in the presence of God on our behalf." (Heb 9:24)

Reflection: The author of the Letter to the Hebrews presumes that Christ is the greatest of all Hebrew Bible (Old Testament) high priests. Just as the high priest had to enter the Holy of Holies—a copy of the heavenly one—of the Jerusalem Temple yearly and make a sacrifice of blood to remove the sins of the chosen people, Jesus entered the heavenly temple, where he offered his own blood to God to remove all sin once for all. In the heavenly temple, Christ is found functioning as the greatest high priest for us.

Christ is found as high priest in our celebration of the Eucharist. As he did upon the cross—offer himself to God—so does he do under the appearance of bread and wine. Through the praying of the Eucharistic Prayer, the priest in the person of Christ asks God to accept the non-bloody sacrifice of the high priest, Christ. Through baptism, a person is incorporated into the priesthood of Christ; he or she is anointed with Chrism Oil to be a priest and to offer himself or herself to God with Christ. Confirmation seals his or her priesthood with the Holy Spirit.

Christ is found as high priest in Penance. Since he has already achieved the forgiveness of sins once for all, he eternally mediates God's remittance of trespasses. Through the Anointing of the Sick, the ill are directed to offer their suffering with Christ to God as they are more and more conformed to the image of the high priest himself.

Christ is found as high priest in Matrimony. As a man gives himself in trust, fidelity, and freedom to a woman, and as the woman gives herself in trust, fidelity, and freedom to a man, they share intimately the Christ they have become through baptism, confirmation, and Eucharist with each other.

As you pray this joyful mystery, reflect on all the ways you have found Christ in the temple of your body, especially through your celebration of the sacraments of the church. Be aware of how you are already sharing in heaven itself because the great high priest, who chooses you for his body, stands before God and intercedes on your behalf. Be joyful that you are found with Christ in the heavenly temple.

2

Luminous Mysteries

Baptism in the Jordan

The Wedding at Cana

Proclamation of the Kingdom of God

The Transfiguration

Institution of the Eucharist

Baptism in the Jordan

Celebrated: Sunday after the Epiphany of the Lord (between January 2 and 6) unless this Sunday occurs on January 7 or 8, then it is celebrated on the following Monday, The Baptism of the Lord.

Option 1

Scripture: "John would have prevented [Jesus from being baptized], saying, 'I need to be baptized by you, and do you come to me?' But Jesus answered him, 'Let it be so now; for it is proper for us in this way to fulfill all righteousness.' Then he consented." (Matt 3:14–15)

Reflection: Because each evangelist after Mark, commonly accepted as the oldest gospel, tries to tone down or erase Jesus' baptism by John, we must conclude that the event caused a problem near the end of the first century. Many were saying that John must be the greater since he did the baptizing.

Luminous Mysteries

The author of Matthew's Gospel deals with the issue by inserting dialogue into the baptismal story he got from Mark's Gospel; biblical scholars concur that Matthew copies most of Mark's Gospel into his own book. Through the dialogue between John the Baptist, who prefers not to baptize Jesus, and Jesus, who instructs John the do it, Jesus emerges as the greater person.

In his version of the story, Matthew uses the occasion to introduce his favorite word: righteousness. He has already given an example of righteousness in the person of Joseph, who breaks the law that pregnant Mary should be stoned by taking her into his home as his wife at the bidding of the angel of the Lord. Jesus further clarifies the meaning of righteousness, indicating that God wills that people do the right thing because they know what the right thing to do is.

Sometimes called the higher righteousness in Matthew's Gospel, the concept refers to going above the letter of the Law or Torah in order to adhere to the principle upon which the Law is based. For example, the Torah forbids adultery, but Jesus declares that lust is adultery in the heart. The Law forbids perjury, but Jesus advocates integrity, which eliminates all swearing of oaths. If the Torah moderates retaliation, Jesus declares that those who follow him should not resist an evildoer but love all their enemies.

In other words, righteousness names the state of life of those who are doing what God wants because they know that it is the right thing to do. They end up keeping the Torah by adhering to the principles upon which the Law is built.

As you pray this mystery of light, reflect upon your deeds of righteousness, those actions that declare that you are a follower of Jesus, those actions that let God's light shine through you.

Option 2

Scripture: "In those days Jesus came from Nazareth of Galilee and was baptized by John in the Jordan." (Mark 1:9)

Reflection: The baptism of Jesus by John the Baptist in the Jordan River is the subject of many stained glass windows, paintings, mosaics, and baptismal font covers. In almost every depiction, John pours water over the head of a standing or kneeling Jesus while a dove hovers above and rays of light pierce the clouds in the sky. However, no one of the four accounts of Jesus' baptism in the Jordan mentions all of that. As is often the case, popular iconography often presents a picture quite different from that painted by words in the gospels.

In Mark's account of Jesus' baptism, there is no doubt that John the Baptist baptizes Jesus. After John baptizes Jesus, Jesus sees the heavens torn apart and the Spirit descend to the earth like a dove. Ancient people conceived of their world as a three-storied universe. God lived on the top level (above the heavens); people lived on the middle floor (earth); and the dead lived on the first floor (under the earth, underworld, netherworld). The torn-apart heavens, then, indicate that God has come to earth and that God's Spirit has entered Jesus, God's Son.

Jesus alone—except, of course, for the reader—hears the voice from heaven declare that he is its Son in whom it is well pleased, quoting from Psalm 2:7. Thus, it is no great revelation that Jesus begins his mission proclaiming, ". . . [The] kingdom of God has come near . . . (Mark 1:15).

Today, the Mighty One's voice comes through human voices, who, like Jesus, proclaim God's activity in our lives. As husbands and wives discern careers, children, buying a house, or buying a car, they can hear the Holy One's voice. Parents are God's voice through the example of the lifestyle they model for their children. Friends, who listen intently, give advice, or comfort, serve as the voice of God. The Merciful One's revelation in our lives through others' voices often is like a beam of light. Suddenly, we recognize that God's reign has come near our lives.

As you pray this mystery of light, reflect on what God has been saying to you through all the enlightening voices in your life.

Option 3

Scripture: "Now when all the people were baptized, and when Jesus also had been baptized and was praying, the heaven was opened, and the Holy Spirit descended upon him in bodily form like a dove." (Luke 3:21–22a)

Reflection: In order to deal with the first-century controversy of whether John the Baptist was greater than Jesus or vice-versa, Luke chooses to elevate Jesus above John the Baptist by removing John from the baptismal scene. Before the author of Luke's Gospel rewrites in passive voice the story he found in Mark's Gospel, he tells how King Herod had John locked up in prison. Thus, there is no doubt that John did not baptize Jesus, according to Luke, because he was in prison before Jesus was baptized. Thus, Jesus is greater than John.

Luke, however, uses the narrative of Jesus non-baptism by John to introduce one of his favorite themes: prayer. Uniquely in Luke's Gospel, Jesus is found praying before every major event in his life. He prays before choosing the twelve apostles. While he is praying, he is transfigured. Jesus prays before he teaches his followers how to pray. He even prays for those who crucify him.

The point of portraying Jesus at prayer is to convince Luke's Gentile readers that prayer—listening to God—is a very important part of a Christian life. Most of the time the focus of prayer is on telling the Holy One what needs to be done from our point of view. Through his portrayal of Jesus at prayer, Luke wants us to realize that prayer is listening to God praying in us and telling us what we need to do.

A life of prayer should begin in one's family even before one is baptized. Parents can pray with their child in the womb before he or she is ever born. After birth and baptism, daily prayer should become as much a part of one's day as eating and sleeping. By listening intently to God, we come to know what it is that the Mighty One asks of us; then, we can do it.

As you pray this mystery of light, reflect on how you pray. If you discover that you tell God what needs to be done, change your prayer to intense listening. Also pay close attention to when you pray and what time of the day is best for you; change that, too, if necessary. Be thankful to God who shines the light of prayer in you.

Option 4

Scripture: [John the Baptist testified,] "I saw the Spirit descending from heaven like a dove, and it remained on [Jesus]. I myself did not know him, but the one who sent me to baptize with water said to me, 'He on whom you see the Spirit descend and remain is the one who baptizes with the Holy Spirit.'" (John 1:32–33)

Reflection: The author of John's Gospel deals with the issue of the superiority of Jesus over John the Baptist by not even narrating the event of Jesus' baptism. After John declares that Jesus existed before him, he proceeds to narrate the non-baptismal event by focusing on the descent of the Holy Spirit upon Jesus like a dove. In John, the descent of the Holy Spirit is a sign that makes Jesus known to John. This also gives John the opportunity to introduce one of his gospel's more important themes: the Holy Spirit.

Often called the Advocate, Paraclete, Comforter, or Helper in John, the Holy Spirit takes Jesus' place. While the presence of the incarnate word on the earth is temporary, the presence of the Holy Spirit is forever. This is why the author of John's Gospel not only reflects deeply upon the role of the Advocate, but he also portrays Jesus giving the Holy Spirit to his disciples on Easter evening by breathing on them. English translation cannot capture the original Greek. The Greek word for Spirit, *pneuma*, can mean wind, breath, and spirit. Thus, Jesus' action of breathing on his disciples might be better rendered as "inspiriting" them.

Only the author of John's Gospel uses this action to connote the gift of the Holy Spirit. The Synoptic Gospels (Matthew, Mark, Luke) use the image of a dove; the author of the Acts of the Apostles combines wind, fire, and speaking in tongues to present the Holy Spirit. And other biblical books use the gesture of the laying on of hands to show how the Paraclete is given to others.

On the day of our baptism, we receive the Holy Spirit through the inspirited water. Through Confirmation, we are sealed with the gift of the Holy Spirit. During the Eucharistic Prayer of the Mass, the priest extends his hands over the bread and wine and calls upon the Holy Spirit to change them into the body and blood of Christ. The Spirit is given through the laying on of hands in Penance, Anointing of the Sick, and Holy Orders.

As you reflect on this mystery, think about the ways the Spirit has descended upon you and how you were filled with light.

The Wedding at Cana

Celebrated: Second Sunday in Ordinary Time, Cycle C

Option 1

Scripture: "On the third day there was a wedding in Cana of Galilee, and the mother of Jesus was there. When the wine gave out, the mother of Jesus said to him, 'They have no wine.' And Jesus said to her, 'Woman, what concern is that to you and to me? My hour has not yet come.'" (John 2:1–4)

Reflection: If all we had were John's Gospel, we would not know the name of the mother of Jesus. Nowhere does the author of John's Gospel name her, because he is not interested in her as a person, but as a sign. Indeed, she is a sign of the church being wedded to God through Jesus.

The mother of Jesus makes but two appearances in John. She is present for the wedding at Cana, a unique Johannine story, and she is present at the cross, another unique Johannine story. In both instances Jesus addresses her as "woman." He never calls her "mother" because that title would distract from her value as a sign.

At Cana she entrusts herself and all those at the wedding to Jesus' concern. At the cross, Jesus entrusts her and all those with her to the apostles in the person of the disciple whom he loved, himself a sign of leadership. While the disciple whom Jesus loved does not appear in the Cana wedding story, he does appear in the narrative of the meal before Passover where he is reclining next to Jesus. Thus, the mother of Jesus and the disciple whom he loved are presented as ideal or model disciples. Jesus' last line in John, "It is finished," indicates that the marriage begun at Cana is now complete. Thus, the mother of Jesus, the church, is present at the beginning and the end of the covenant-making ceremony.

When the mother of Jesus tells him that the wedding party has run out of wine, he declares that his hour has not yet come. Throughout John's Gospel, Jesus refers to his death and resurrection as his hour. Indeed, before he is arrested to begin his suffering, death, and resurrection, he declares that the hour has come.

The author of John's Gospel uses the signs of the mother of Jesus and the disciple whom Jesus loved to spark faith in others. Likewise, many people in our lives are signs that spark faith in us. As you pray this mystery, think about some of those people—mother, father, uncle, aunt, nun, priest, best friend, etc. Reflect on the light each person shed upon your life that enabled you to believe more deeply in Jesus, the incarnate Word of God.

Luminous Mysteries

Option 2

Scripture: "Jesus did . . . the first of his signs, in Cana of Galiee, and revealed his glory; and his disciples believed in him." (John 2:11)

Reflection: The unique narrative of the wedding at Cana is the first of Jesus' seven major signs in John's Gospel which spark belief in his disciples. The basic Johannine scenario for each of the signs involves an event, a miraculous deed done by Jesus, and the ensuing faith of those who are present. As is often the case in John's Gospel, a sign always points to some other reality.

The wedding at Cana is no ordinary marriage. In fact, in John's Gospel, this story begins Jesus' ministerial journey of revealing and wedding God to people which will reach a crescendo at the cross. From the opening line of the story, indicating that it takes place on the third day, the astute reader knows this is a theophany, a manifestation of God through Jesus. No bride is ever mentioned, but the church is present in the sign of the unnamed mother of Jesus. And there are six stone water jars, an incomplete number. All of the meanings of those signs will become clearer at the cross.

The Johannine wedding metaphor can be employed by all who are on a pilgrimage to wholeness. It takes a lifetime to integrate or wed all our human aspects: mental, physical, sexual, psychological, emotional, spiritual, and aesthetic. But time and time again we get a glimpse of such wholeness in a mystic moment of wedded bliss. It may come after finishing a good book or a strenuous workout. It may appear after agonizing over and then solving a problem or understanding an emotional dilemma in a new way. Through each's sharing of self, a married man and woman enact wholeness in their lives. The individual feeling of wholeness is a sign that God is being revealed and more deeply wed to us in and through our lives.

After the steward tastes the water that has become wine, he declares to the bridegroom that he has kept the good wine for last. Indeed, the good wine is Jesus, who gives his life to seal the marriage between God and people.

As you pray this mystery, reflect on the key moments of wedding, when you have experienced wholeness, and, therefore, God, in your life. The way to be sure that the Holy One was present is to look for the light, the glory, that leads you to deeper faith in Jesus.

Option 3

Scripture: ". . . Standing near the cross of Jesus were his mother, and his mother's sister, Mary the wife of Clopas, and Mary Magdalene. [Jesus said,] 'I am thirsty.' A jar full of sour wine was standing there. So [the soldiers] put a sponge full of the wine on a branch of hyssop and held it to his mouth." (John 19:25, 28–29)

Reflection: In John's Gospel, the story of the wedding at Cana begins Jesus' ministerial journey of revealing and wedding God to people which reaches a crescendo at the cross. Just like the wedding occurred on the third day, so the narrative of the cross contains a reference to three women named Mary to indicate that another theophany is taking place.

At the cross we find the unnamed mother of Jesus making her second and final appearance in the gospel; here we find the missing seventh jar of wine (there were only six at Cana); and here we find the church-bride, created from water and blood flowing out of the side of the new Adam, Christ. Just as Eve was created from a rib taken from Adam's side, so the sacraments of baptism (water) and Eucharist (blood) are borne from the side of Christ.

The cross weds heaven to earth; through the new Adam and his bride, God re-creates all. The wedding begun at Cana is completed on the cross. Thus, the wedding at Cana and the cross serve as covers for John's Gospel; what goes on in between is the gradual merger of God and people through Jesus.

The wedding at Cana is a sign for us. God is present when weddings are occurring in our lives. They don't have to be ordinary weddings, because Cana was no ordinary wedding. Sometimes people refer to the wedding as all the pieces of a plan coming together. Other times people talk about surgery and how several doctors transplanted organs or did bypass heart surgery or prepared skin grafts and the patient was made whole again. The wedding may occur deep down within us as we integrate and re-integrate our values in our daily lives and see the results in our personal integrity. Notice that the wedding always involves some form of the cross, some dying to self, so that new life can emerge.

As you pray this mystery, reflect upon the weddings in your life, and particularly note the crosses associated with each. The light that shines through your weddings always culminates with the cross uniting earth and heaven.

Option 4

Scripture: "Let us rejoice and exult and give [the Lord our God] glory, for the marriage of the Lamb has come, and his bride has made herself ready...." (Rev 19:7)

Reflection: While not connected to the Johannine story of the wedding at Cana in Galilee, the Book of Revelation's poem about the marriage of the Lamb contains the same, basic idea: Through the death and resurrection of Christ, God and people have been united in covenant, much like a man and woman are wedded. Revelation portrays Jesus, the Lamb, who was dead and raised to life, as the groom, and the people who have remained faithful throughout persecution as his bride. The bride is dressed in fine, bright, pure linen, representing the righteous deeds of the Lamb's faithful followers.

Just as Jesus manifested his glory at Cana of Galilee in the first of his signs in John's Gospel, so is his glory manifest in the Book of Revelation through the image of a wedding. Those who have held fast to their faith are invited to the wedding supper of the Lamb. Those who have not succumbed to evil share in the Eucharist and collectively form the church, the bride, who, through feasting on the body and blood of the Lamb, is married to the groom, Christ, in an everlasting covenant.

This mystery of the rosary invites us to reflect deeply on our own status as bride of the Lamb. We bring our personal relationship with Christ to the community every Sunday. Our personal relationship not only nourishes us individually, but it also contributes to the growth of all the others members of the church, locally manifested in our parish. Whatever each of us does individually as a bride affects the whole church. That's why we often hear our leaders speak about our ongoing spiritual growth and its affect on the community.

Whatever praying we do throughout the week as an individual member of the bride is brought to the marriage supper, Eucharist, on Sunday. Whatever service we have given throughout the week is brought to Sunday Mass. The individual gifts we use to build up the church are brought to our weekly wedding celebration, where they are further enhanced by all others who are, likewise, bringing their prayer, service, and talents to share with us.

As you pray this mystery, reflect upon all the ways you live your bride status in relationship to all other brides in your parish. And give God glory for the light that shines through you and through your community as the bride of the Lamb.

Proclamation of the Kingdom of God

Luminous Mysteries

Celebrated: Third Sunday in Ordinary Time, Cycles A, B, and C

Option 1

Scripture: "Now when Jesus heard that John had been arrested, he withdrew to Galilee. From that time Jesus began to proclaim, 'Repent, for the kingdom of heaven has come near.'" (Matt 4:12, 17)

Reflection: In Matthew's Gospel, both John the Baptist and Jesus preach the same message. Both sound like the prophets in their call to people to return to God or to change the direction of their lives. In the past, the prophets' call to return to the Holy One was based on the people failing to keep the terms of the covenant. Now, the cause for returning to God or changing the direction of life is the nearness of the kingdom of heaven. The author of Matthew's Gospel does not use Mark's "kingdom of God"; he changes the phrase to "kingdom of heaven" out of respect for the divine name.

Once Jesus takes up John the Baptist's message, he begins to enact the kingdom of heaven. Through his ministry as healer, teacher, preacher, feeder, etc., Jesus gives a foretaste of what the fullness of the kingdom will be. The future and final salvation of all humankind is achieved only through the reign of God, who establishes justice and peace. There is no talk of a "new covenant" in Matthew's Gospel because Jesus' message expands on the covenant; it does not change it. Thus, returning in Matthew means that people recognize what God is doing through Jesus to establish his kingdom on earth.

Indeed, what is God doing in our lives to establish his reign of justice and peace on the earth? And what change do we need to make in our lives to enable that to occur? Just as God worked through Jesus of Nazareth in the past, so now God works through us who believe that he is the Messiah, the Savior of the world. Because the fullness of the kingdom is not yet realized, we still get only glimmers of it.

For example, the kingdom of heaven comes near us when we engage in healing others. We don't have to be doctors to heal; healing occurs when we listen to one who is grieving, when we console one who is divorced, when we visit the sick in hospitals, nursing homes, or in their own homes. We experience the kingdom when we teach children about our faith or tutor them in basic skills, when we feed the hungry through donations of food or serving in a soup kitchen.

As you pray this mystery, reflect upon all the ways that the kingdom of heaven is revealed in your life. Be aware that this light is only a dim reflection of the fullness that awaits you.

Option 2

Scripture: "Now after John was arrested, Jesus came to Galilee, proclaiming the good news of God, and saying, 'The time is fulfilled, and the kingdom of God has come near; repent, and believe in the good news.'" (Mark 1:14–15)

Reflection: In Mark's Gospel, the kingdom of God comes with two major events. The first is that of the baptism of Jesus when the heavens are torn apart. Using the concept of a three-storied universe with the notion that God lives above the heavens, the author of Mark's Gospel is portraying God falling to the earth.

The second occurs immediately after Jesus dies when the curtain in the Temple is torn in two from top to bottom. Using the concept that God lives in the Holy of Holies of the Temple, Mark is saying that God gets out.

Thus, Jesus' proclamation of the gospel, the good news of God's victory, is that through Jesus and his ministry, God has established a reign on the earth. In other words, the Holy One is no longer located above the dome of the sky nor in the Holy of Holies; now, God is near people.

The response demanded to the Mighty One's nearness requires repentance and faith in the gospel. Repentance means that we change our minds about something; in Mark the change of mind has to do with God's presence or nearness. Before Jesus, the Holy One was located above the dome of the sky and in the inner sanctuary of the Temple. Mark challenges his readers to change their minds about those presuppositions; the author wants people to realize that God is with people.

Professing faith in the gospel means that we believe in the good news of the victory, namely, that through the suffering and death of Jesus, God has drawn near to people. The Mighty One did not fight a battle or destroy the enemy; the Holy One chose to be with people in the person of Jesus of Nazareth.

As you pray this mystery, reflect upon the ways that God has come near to you. Notice how your response to the Holy One's light sparks repentance in you and deeper faith in God.

Option 3

Scripture: "... Jesus, filled with the power of the Spirit, returned to Galilee, and a report about him spread through all the surrounding country. He began to teach in their synagogues and was praised by everyone." (Luke 4:14–15)

Reflection: The author of Luke's Gospel does not portray Jesus inaugurating his ministry by proclaiming the nearness of God's kingdom or the kingdom of heaven as do Matthew and Mark, respectively. Instead, Luke chooses to present Jesus delivering his first sermon in the synagogue in Nazareth after he reads from the prophet Isaiah. The words of Isaiah establish the outline for the rest of Luke's Gospel. Jesus, the Spirit-conceived child, the Anointed One, will bring good news to the poor, proclaim release to captives, proclaim recovery of sight to the blind, let the oppressed go free, and proclaim the year of God's favor. As he goes about fulfilling the words of Isaiah, Jesus is motivated and guided by the Spirit.

The Lukan Jesus' mission is also our own. Because we are anointed with the Holy Spirit in Baptism and Confirmation, we are sent to serve the poor. Volunteering in the local St. Vincent de Paul Society center, serving on a fair housing board, or meeting the needs of the homeless may be ways we accomplish our mission to serve the poor.

We proclaim release to captives when we speak out against harsh penalties for crimes, the death sentence, and improper treatment of inmates. While we may not at first think that we can proclaim sight to the blind, we can read to those who cannot see, we can provide audio recordings to them, and we can mentor those in after-school, sports, and other types of programs.

The depressed may need only a few minutes of our time to be set free of their oppression. Those confined to wheel chairs may need only a little push to get out of their homes and be released from their oppression. Working with at-risk teens can be a means of setting free oppression that we may never know about. And every year we have is one of God's favor. We are still alive to do God's work.

As you pray this mystery, reflect upon how you continue the mission of Jesus to bring good news to the poor, to proclaim release to captives, to proclaim recovery of sight to the blind, to let the oppressed go free, and to proclaim the year of God's favor. Notice the light that your spread.

Option 4

Scripture: [Jesus said,] "The kingdom of God is not coming with things that can be observed; nor will they say, 'Look, here it is!' or 'There it is!' For, in fact, the kingdom of God is among you." (Luke 17:20–21)

Reflection: It matters little how it is phrased; even though each evangelist puts his own spin on Jesus' message that the kingdom of God is among us. The basic concept that God is with people here and now serves as Jesus' basic proclamation. Especially true in Luke's Gospel is the fact that Jesus enacts God's reign primarily through parables.

God is everywhere people are, declares Jesus. Such is not a radical concept to us today. But for ancient people who "located" God above the vault in the heavens or in the Holy of Holies of the Temple, Jesus' declaration that God was among them was very hard to take. His preaching identified God's reign as present; it is not some type of life to look forward to after death. It is not some eternal reward or punishment. God's reign is among us.

Of course, it is much easier to turn the presence of God into a distant longing and tone down Jesus' basic message. Despite the fact that religious people talk a lot about seeking God, they would prefer that the Always-present One stay out of their business!

God cannot be so controlled, even by technicians of the sacred. God's reign erupts like light from deep within us. When we see the injustice of a living wage and speak out against and work toward changing the system that keeps others locked in it, God's kingdom is among us. When we speak the truth in the midst of corporate stealing and lying and fraud, God's kingdom is among us. Just treating every person with basic human dignity by refusing to engage in racism, sexism, or religious discrimination reveals God's kingdom among us. In those special moments, we take over where Jesus left off and enact God's kingdom here and now. That is why Christianity is a way of life; it is the way one lives in the kingdom now. It is how we live in God's present moment.

As he went about proclaiming God's kingdom, Jesus gathered followers who represented the kind of people in which God was interested. The poor, prostitutes, tax collectors, lepers, the lost, inept fishermen, the diseased—they were ushered into God's reign. The interest continues today through those who continue to proclaim God's kingdom among us. As you pray this mystery of light, reflect upon the times that God's kingdom has erupted from deep within you.

The Transfiguration

Celebrated: August 6, The Transfiguration of the Lord, and the Second Sunday of Lent, Cycles A, B, and C

Option 1

Scripture: ". . . [Jesus] was transfigured before [Peter, James, and John], and his face shone like the sun, and his clothes became dazzling white." (Matt 17:2)

Reflection: In each gospel, the story of Jesus' metamorphosis has a different meaning, depending upon its location in the story. Matthew alters the transfiguration narrative he found in Mark by envisioning it as a revelatory event of epic proportions predicting the post-resurrection appearances Jesus makes at the end of the gospel.

According to the author of Matthew's Gospel, God reveals the Holy One through Jesus. Notice that the verb is always passive; Jesus was transfigured, not he transfigured himself. What the gospel writer describes as happening only once actually took place many times in Jesus' life, especially as he preached the higher righteousness, doing the right thing because it is the right thing to do. God's light shone through him, and Jesus cooperated with that light throughout his life.

Matthew portrays Jesus as coming to see that his mission to the lost sheep of the house of Israel has to be expanded to the nations of the world. By the time Matthew is penning his gospel, the Gentiles are becoming believers and need to be incorporated into the new people God has chosen.

Just as God transfigured Jesus, so the Mighty One transfigures, sparks change, throughout your life. God's light breaks through in love shared and consecrated by husband and wife and all the interchange that occurs throughout their marriage. It shines through children and grandchildren causing parents and grandparents to change their lives. The glow of a sunrise or sunset may evoke a transformation. Walking through a park, the woods, a meadow, or a flower garden can send a blare of beauty that leaves one altered. Even embers kindled in a fireplace can produce a brightness that fills one with insight and alters thought patterns.

As you pray this mystery of light, reflect on all the changes God has worked in your life and how God's brilliance has left you changed forever, never again to be the same. Be prepared, like Jesus, to be dazzled.

Option 2

Scripture: "Six days later, Jesus took with him Peter and James and John, and led them up a high mountain apart, by themselves. And he was transfigured before them, and his clothes became dazzling white, such as no one on earth could bleach them." (Mark 9:2–3)

Reflection: For the author of Mark's Gospel, transfiguration is another way to attempt to describe resurrection; since the original ending of Mark gives no post-resurrection appearances of Jesus, Mark tells us that resurrection is like being changed into white light while speaking with the two long-dead heroes, Moses and

Elijah. In other words, the transfiguration story in Mark's Gospel serves as a post-resurrection account, too. That would seem to be clear from the appearance of Moses and Elijah.

The transfiguration in Mark also confirms the turning point in the gospel. Up to this point in the story, Jesus has been portrayed as a man powerful in deed and word. Immediately before the transfiguration narrative, he has begun to teach his disciples about powerlessness, especially the powerlessness of taking up the cross and following him. The voice heard from the cloud is a parallel to the voice from the torn-apart heavens in Jesus' baptismal scene. Whereas only Jesus heard the voice after his baptism, now Peter, James, and John hear the voice declaring that Jesus is God's Son to whom they need to listen.

Throughout the second half of Mark's Gospel, the theme of powerless discipleship predominates. Two more times Jesus talks about his own powerless death. Interspersed are stories about how those who want to be first have to be last, how one must be powerless, like a child, to enter God's kingdom, and how those who are rich must sell all they have and give it away to the poor.

Because we live in a culture that fosters personal power at every step of our lives, this is a difficult mystery to pray. To be transfigured, according to Mark, means that first we have to be powerless so that God can shed new light on us. As you pray this mystery of light, reflect on the ways that worldly power corrupts you, and ask God to help you become a powerless follower of Jesus by taking up your cross and following him.

Option 3

Scripture: "[Moses and Elijah] appeared in glory and were speaking of [Jesus'] departure, which he was about to accomplish at Jerusalem." (Luke 9:31)

Reflection: Like Matthew before him, the author of Luke's Gospel rewrites the story of the transfiguration he found in Mark by portraying it as an opportunity to explain Jesus' journey to Jerusalem, where he will make his departure, exodus, through death to perfect new life. Luke also records several post-resurrection appearances to prove that there is life on the other side of the grave. Of course Jesus' journey to Jerusalem can't stop there. His mission must be delegated to the next generation of Gentiles after the evangelization efforts of the heroic apostles, Peter and Paul.

The exodus metaphor is an old one, employed repeatedly throughout the Hebrew Bible (Old Testament). Of course, there is THE exodus of God's chosen people out of the slavery of Egypt to the promised land. That exodus was led by Moses. The metaphor is even read backward into the account of the journey of Abraham and Sarah from Ur in Babylon to the promised land. Joshua re-enacts the exodus at the Jordan River as do the prophets Elijah and Elisha. And Isaiah employs the metaphor when writing about the exodus of the Jews from Babylonian captivity and their return to the land of Israel.

To be transfigured is to make an exodus. For Luke that exodus is to pass through death to resurrected life and, then, to ascend into heaven to be with Moses and Elijah in glory. While we have to wait for our final exodus, our Christian lifetime pilgrimage should include many of them. For example, we may have changed our way of prayer over the years. It is always a fearful endeavor to alter the way we pray, but if there is no growth in prayer forms, then we may be stuck and need an exodus.

What began as an image of marriage is changed by the man and woman who entered into the covenant relationship. Both grow into their marriage and shape it accordingly. If there is no exodus from past understandings, then the union becomes stale and dies. It takes a lot of "exodusing" to keep a marriage fresh and alive.

As you pray this mystery, reflect on your own exoduses. Name the times you had to journey on and leave part of yourself behind so that you could be changed into someone new. As you do so, notice all the light that has been shining through the changes in your life.

Option 4

Scripture: "[Our Lord Jesus Christ] received honor and glory from God the Father when that voice was conveyed to him by the Majestic Glory, saying, 'This is my Son, my Beloved, with whom I am well pleased.'" (2 Pet 1:17)

Reflection: Other than the references to the Transfiguration in Matthew, Mark, and Luke, there is the mention of it in the Second Letter of Peter. The unknown author of Second Peter, who writes in the name of the apostle, makes clear that he was on the holy mountain with Jesus and heard the voice. Whoever the author of the letter is, he used Matthew's Gospel as his source for the words of the voice, since both Mark and Luke use different words.

The words of the voice employed by Matthew and Second Peter are the combination of two Hebrew Bible (Old Testament) verses. The first comes from Psalm 2:7, a royal coronation song, which portrays God as adopting the new Judean king as the LORD's son. As such, the new king represents the Holy One's universal reign. The second comes from the prophet Isaiah's first of four servant poems in which the servant is introduced as a royal emissary being presented at court. Thus, Matthew, and consequently Second Peter, portrays Jesus as God's Son and emissary to the world upon whom is bestowed the Holy One's own authority.

The author of Second Peter reinterprets the meaning of the transfiguration as an event that predicts Jesus' return in glory to judge the world. By the time of the writing of this letter early in the second century, the hope for Christ's return was beginning to wane. After all, Paul had thought that he would see the day of Jesus' coming again, but he died not witnessing it. Second Peter attempts to shore up the hope that Christ will return to judge the world.

Two thousand years later we still await the coming in glory of Christ. It is an aspect of our Christian faith that can easily get overlooked. The church uses part of the season of Advent to focus on the Son's return in glory, but it should be a part of our daily lives. So, as you pray this mystery of light, focus on the hope required to maintain the expectation that Jesus will come again. At every Mass in the Profession of Faith (Creed) we declare our belief that Christ will come again in glory to judge the living and the dead, and, after the Our Father, we acknowledge that we await the blessed hope and the coming of our Savior, Jesus Christ.

Institution of the Eucharist

Celebrated: Holy Thursday Evening Mass of the Lord's Supper and Sunday after the Most Holy Trinity, The Most Holy Body and Blood of Christ (Corpus Christi)

Option 1

Scripture: "While they were eating, Jesus took a loaf of bread, and after blessing it he broke it, gave it to the disciples, and said, 'Take, eat; this is my body.' Then he took a cup, and after giving thanks he gave it to them, saying, 'Drink from it, all of you; for this is my blood of the covenant, which is poured out for many for the forgiveness of sins.'" (Matt 26:26–28)

Reflection: Like the author of Mark's Gospel, the author of Matthew's Gospel views Jesus' death through the lens of a Passover meal. He also understands Jesus' death to be a covenant in continuity with the shedding of blood through circumcision with Abraham and the sprinkling of the blood of bulls on the chosen people with Moses.

However, the author of Matthew's Gospel declares that Jesus' death is for the forgiveness of sins. Jesus' sacrifice on the cross has atoning, saving significance. In Jewish understanding, the life of a person or animal was in its blood. So, Jesus offers his own blood to God to save all people. Furthermore, the Matthean Jesus possesses the authority to command that his followers eat and drink, and, thus, participate in the life of the covenant he is extending to all people.

No longer do we think that blood contains all of life. We know that a healthy body consists of many different organs functioning together and kept alive through the blood that both brings nutrients to the cells of those organs and transports waste from those organs. But even with such knowledge, we still think that life is flowing out of us when we cut our finger and see bright red blood begin to ooze out. Likewise, we speak about sharing the gift of life when we give blood. And not to be missed is the importance of blood transfusions which keep critically injured people alive.

When we celebrate the Eucharist and observe Jesus' command to eat and drink, we eat and drink of his sacrificial life, which, in a non-bloody manner, is offered to God again and again for the forgiveness of sins of the world. His body and blood give life to us both here and now and eternal life in the world to come.

As you pray this mystery of light, name the ways that you have shared blood with others. And be aware of how your sacrifice continues the one Jesus began on the cross.

Option 2

Scripture: "While [Jesus and his disciples] were eating, he took a loaf of bread, and after blessing it he broke it, gave it to them, and said, 'Take; this is my body.' Then he took a cup and after giving thanks he gave it to them, and all of them drank from it. He said to them, 'This is my blood of the covenant, which is poured out for many.'" (Mark 14:22–24)

Reflection: Most catholics are more familiar with the narrative they hear in the Eucharistic Prayer during Mass than they are with the four distinct versions of the Lord's Supper in the Christian Bible (New Testament) because the Eucharistic Prayer formula is a synthesis of the four versions.

The author of Mark's Gospel interprets the meaning of Jesus' death through the lens of the Jewish feast of Passover. Mark understands Jesus' death to be in continuity with the covenant God entered into with Abraham through the blood of circumcision and Moses through the sprinkling of the blood of bulls. Thus, in Mark's Gospel, Jesus' death is a sacrifice for others.

As do the other accounts, Mark's version of the Lord's Supper features common food staples of the ancient world: bread and wine. The bread would have been unleavened, coarse, round, flat loaves. The wine would have been little more than fermented grape juice cut with water. The result of people together eating bread and drinking wine—unity—is the reverse of the process of making those staples. Many individual grains of wheat are ground together to make flour. Many individual grapes are squeezed together to get juice to make wine. Just as the many grains become one loaf and the many grapes become one wine, so the many diners become one. In other words, when people eat and drink together, they enter into a unity which the Lord's Supper discloses as the real presence of God in Christ, both through the elements and through the diners.

We don't realize how often we enact this mystery. When families and friends gather for Thanksgiving dinner, Christmas lunch, Easter brunch, and birthday and anniversary commemorations, they may eat turkey, ham, or beef, but the staples of bread and wine are present in some form. Through the action of eating and drinking together, the diners renew the ties that bind them.

As you pray this mystery of light, reflect on the unifying experiences you have had through the staples of bread and wine and give thanks to God for them.

Option 3

Scripture: "Then [Jesus] took a loaf of bread, and when he had given thanks, he broke it and gave it to [the apostles], saying, 'This is my body, which is given for you. Do this in remembrance of me.' And he did the same with the cup after supper, saying, 'This cup that is poured out for you is the new covenant in my blood.'" (Luke 22:19–20)

Reflection: The author of Luke's Gospel understands that Jesus' death creates a new covenant. Situating the Last Supper more within the context of a Passover meal—by narrating Jesus' taking of two cups of wine—Luke portrays Jesus taking the bread like the head of a household, breaking it, and distributing it to those at his table as a sign that he is able to provide for his own family. Jesus takes the bread, breaks it, and declares that he will provide himself, his own body, for his followers.

Not only is Luke echoing the Exodus covenant renewal with the bulls' blood sprinkled on the people by Moses, but he is also referring to the covenant the prophet Jeremiah said would be written on people's hearts. Jesus' blood establishes a new covenant for the salvation of all people.

Luke's narrative of the Lord's Supper brings together two themes that he was woven throughout his gospel. The first is that of Jesus as one who eats meals with all people—sinners and saints. No gospel portrays Jesus eating meals more than Luke; in fact, there is no chapter in Luke's Gospel that does not have some direct or indirect reference to food.

The second theme woven into the Last Supper narrative is that of the birth of the new Israel. Luke understands that the old

Israel, usually signified by the Temple, gives birth to the new Israel, signified by the Twelve and those who follow Jesus. That's why the Lukan Jesus says that the cup contains the blood of the new covenant.

Luke's Passover setting for Jesus' last meal with his apostles celebrates the Jewish liberation from slavery. It also celebrates the freeing of all people from whatever enslaves them.

As you pray this mystery of light, reflect upon what might enslave you: commercialism, individualism, materialism, etc. As you name your slavery, remember that you have been set free through the blood of the new covenant established by Christ.

Option 4

Scripture: "... [T]he Lord Jesus on the night when he was betrayed took a loaf of bread, and when he had given thanks, he broke it and said, 'This is my body that is for you. Do this in remembrance of me.' In the same way he took the cup also, after supper, saying, 'This cup is the new covenant in my blood. Do this, as often as you drink it, in remembrance of me.' For as often as you eat this bread and drink the cup, you proclaim the Lord's death until he comes." (1 Cor 11:23-26)

Reflection: Because Paul thinks that he will see the day when Christ will return, he understands the Lord's Supper to be a meal that proclaims Jesus' death until he comes again. Catholics are familiar with that position because that line is the basis for one of the Memorial Acclamations used during Mass.

Paul's emphasis is on remembering the death of Christ. Unique to his narrative of the Last Supper, he adds Jesus' words about remembering him by both breaking the bread and drinking from the cup. In other words, the broken bread should remind those celebrating the Lord's Supper that Jesus' body was broken for them. And drinking from the cup should remind them that his blood was poured out for them in a new covenant. As they remember his broken body and poured-out blood in death, they await his return in glory.

Every Eucharist we celebrate contains Paul's focus on remembering. After the priest or bishop recalls the words of institution with the bread and cup, he continues with prayers that remember Jesus' suffering, death, resurrection, and ascension. We call to mind the great events that brought us salvation in Christ.

As catholics, we remember this great event of the past because it becomes present for us on our altar. What Jesus did on the night he was betrayed—give himself as food and drink—he continues to do today. Through the action of the Holy Spirit, the bread and wine become the body and blood of Christ which we share. In our act of sharing the broken body and poured-out blood of Christ, we are united to Christ and each other—since we are all members of his body. Thus, the Last Supper of Jesus becomes the ever-present supper of Christ with us.

As you pray this mystery of light, reflect on the meaning of the acclamation that when we eat the bread and drink the cup, we proclaim the death of Christ until he comes.

3

Sorrowful Mysteries

The Agony in the Garden

The Scourging at the Pillar

The Crowning with Thorns

The Carrying of the Cross

The Crucifixion

The Agony in the Garden

Celebrated: Palm Sunday of the Passion of the Lord

Option 1

Scripture: "[Jesus] took with him Peter and the two sons of Zebedee, and began to be grieved and agitated. Then he said to them, 'I am deeply grieved, even to death; remain here, and stay awake with me.'" (Matt 26:37–38)

Reflection: In Matthew's narrative of Jesus' agony in Gethsemane, the focus is on the betrayal that is about to be enacted by both Judas and Peter. The author of Matthew's Gospel refines the Judas character he got from Mark's Gospel by making him more dastardly and deadly. He betrays Jesus to the Jewish authorities for thirty pieces of silver. Then, after he realizes that he has betrayed innocent blood, he betrays himself by hanging himself.

Following Mark's lead, Matthew portrays Peter betraying Jesus three times, but the Matthean Peter weeps bitterly in repentance.

Sorrowful Mysteries

Matthew understands Peter to be the rock upon which the church is built. So, he gives Peter status by enabling him to walk on water with Jesus, and by portraying Jesus calling him a rock and giving to him the keys to the kingdom of heaven. Peter appears at the end of Matthew's Gospel and is given the mission to go teach and baptize the nations.

Peter is contrasted with Judas in Matthew's Gospel. Peter repents of his betrayal, but Judas does not. Peter repents by weeping bitterly. Judas fails to repent, and ends up betraying himself through suicide.

Jesus' agony in Gethsemane in Matthew's Gospel gives hope to those who are betrayed. Nightly, on the evening news, we hear stories of betrayal. A teacher betrays a student entrusted to his or her care. One partner in a marriage betrays his or her spouse. A parent betrays a child, or a child betrays a parent. Even our most-trusted clergy have been found guilty of betrayal of those they were committed to serve.

As you pray this sorrowful mystery, reflect on your own experiences of betrayal. They may have included the betrayal of a friendship, the telling of a secret, the politics of confusion, etc. Name whatever betrayals you have lived with in your lifetime. Ask God to help you drink the cup of betrayal. If you were the betrayer, be sorrowful, repent, and trust in God's forgiveness.

Option 2

Scripture: [Jesus] . . . began to be distressed and agitated. And he said to [Peter, James, and John], 'I am deeply grieved, even to death; remain here, and keep awake.'" (Mark 14:33–34)

Reflection: In Mark's Gospel, Jesus is portrayed as distressed and agitated in Gethsemane. He prays three times to the Father, asking him to remove the cup because the tragedy of his suffering and death is quickly approaching.

We spend a lot of time avoiding the suffering and dying that are intricately attached to living. More energy can be spent circumventing suffering and dying than is needed to walk through them. So, we procrastinate projects at home because doing them means giving up some TV or movie time or some other pleasurable activities. A relationship that is not mutually nourishing for both persons just continues rather than one person facing the other and calling him or her to accountability. Employers complain that they get fewer hours of work from employees, who find more and more distractions, like cell phones, personal calls, days off, etc., because they don't face the work and finish it. Students in high school and college often put off homework and paper-writing until the last possible moment in an effort to avoid the agony of completing assignments.

The word *agony* means *anguish*, *struggle*, or *intense pain*. Being a human being, Jesus experiences anguish when faced with the prospect of his own suffering and death. He struggles to do God's will. And he experiences both the mental and the physical pain of dying on a cross. He serves as a model of how to face the agony and follow the path through it instead of finding ways to avoid it. He trusts that God's presence will sustain him through the agony and enrich his life because of it.

As you pray this sorrowful mystery, reflect on your own experiences both of putting off agony and going through it. In which ones did you experience the presence of God? How was your life enriched?

Option 3

Scripture: "Then [Jesus] withdrew from [the disciples] about a stone's throw, knelt down, and prayed, 'Father, if you are willing, remove this cup from me; yet, not my will but yours be done.' In his anguish he prayed more earnestly, and his sweat become like great drops of blood falling down on the ground." (Luke 22:41–42, 44)

Reflection: In Luke's telling of the agony in the garden story, a sweating-blood Jesus prays only once on the Mount of Olives. Jesus has been portrayed as a pray-er throughout Luke's Gospel. Before every major event in his life, he has been found at prayer, such as his baptism, before naming twelve apostles, before teaching the

Our Father, etc. So, it comes as no surprise that Luke portrays Jesus at prayer before he is betrayed by Judas.

Also, Luke mentions that an angel came to strengthen him as he prepares for his innocent martyrdom. Unique to Luke's telling of the rest of the passion story, Jesus is declared innocent of any crime by Pilate, Herod, one of the two criminals, and the centurion. Jesus dies a martyr, a witness to the life he has led and taught about to others.

Luke's account of the agony on the Mount of Olives reminds us that doing God's will involves suffering for Jesus—and for us. His prayer does not ask God to remove suffering; his prayer asks God to remove suffering only if it is the Father's will. The cup of suffering, like the cross, is never too heavy to bear, however. For Jesus, God sends an angel to strengthen him. And, if we look around, we might be surprised at all the unrecognized angels God sends to us to strengthen us in our suffering.

For example, the angel who strengthened you after surgery may have been a nurse or several different nurses. They looked in on you. They dressed your sutures, they bathed or assisted you to bathe, they gave you drink and food. Your angel may have been a neighbor who brought you cookies and words of support after a family tragedy. A few words spoken by a clerk in a store can be angelic sounds that enable us to get through the shopping of the day.

As you pray this sorrowful mystery, name the angels in your life who have strengthened you in your suffering. Be thankful to God for having sent an angel to help you drink from the cup and do the Father's will.

Option 4

Scripture: "I am now rejoicing in my sufferings for your sake, and in my flesh I am completing what is lacking in Christ's afflictions for the sake of his body, that is, the church." (Col 1:24)

Reflection: In a culture that despises suffering and does everything in its power to eradicate it, the words of the author of the Letter to the Colossians will be difficult, if not impossible, to read or hear. Our solution to suffering is to drug it, excise it, or kill it, because we see it as an unnecessary evil.

In Colossians, second-generation Paul sees agony as a means of maturity. Suffering is necessary if we are to grow into the image of Christ, who, through his own suffering and death, showed us how to do God's will. It is not that anything is lacking in what Jesus suffered; it is that while we await his return in glory, we mature and come closer to the day of his arrival.

Our agony is not for ourselves; that would be narcissistic. Our suffering is for the good of the other members of the body, the church. The woman who suffers with breast cancer can undergo surgery and chemotherapy treatments alone, or she can unite herself with the whole church and contribute to every person's growth in Christ. The man undergoing prostate surgery can be focused solely on himself, or he can view his suffering as assisting all the members of the body of Christ to progress in maturity.

Even a good headache can be the occasion for one to build up the church. Any suffering that we have experienced gives us the grace to sympathize with others who are undergoing the same type of agony. Add in mental or psychological or emotional suffering and it is not hard to conclude that we have multiple opportunities to complete what is lacking in Christ's suffering in order to further his coming in glory. This is not to imply that we should not relieve our suffering when possible; it does imply that we may need to change our cultural attitude about it.

Second-generation Paul rejoices in his suffering. He tells the Colossians that he is happy to suffer for them because his agony will help them mature. As you pray this sorrowful mystery, reflect upon all the suffering that has changed you as it changed Christ. If you have not done so before, view it from the perspective of being for others so that it assists them in reaching maturity, that is, building up the church.

Sorrowful Mysteries

The Scourging at the Pillar

Celebrated: Palm Sunday of the Passion of the Lord and Friday of the Passion of the Lord (Good Friday)

Option 1

Scripture: ". . . Pilate . . . took some water and washed his hands before the crowd, saying, 'I am innocent of [Jesus'] blood; see to it yourselves.' . . . He released Barabbas for them; and after flogging Jesus, he handed him over to be crucified." (Matt 27:24, 26)

Reflection: As in Mark's Gospel, Pilate in Matthew's Gospel realizes that it is out of jealousy that the Jewish officials hand over Jesus to him. However, the author of Matthew's Gospel adds that Pilate feared that the crowd was going to riot. Thinking that Jesus has done no evil, Pilate proceeds, symbolically, to wash his hands of the affair. However, no matter how well Matthew attempts to take the blame off of Pilate, history records that only the Roman governor could sentence a man to crucifixion—which is exactly what Pilate does.

By the 80s CE—when Matthew's Gospel is penned—Jewish Christianity is waning and Gentile Christianity is spreading. Even though Matthew's Gospel is very Jewish, many of his characters are Gentile believers. And in order to facilitate the faith of even more Gentiles, he plays up Gentiles and plays down Jews. By the time Matthew is finished with Gentile Pilate, he looks nothing like the ruthless governor recorded in history.

Sometimes, however, we imitate Pilate. We wash our hands of our responsibilities. For example, parents can wash their hands of their responsibility to guide their children in the practice of their faith and religious education. Who hasn't heard a parent say to a sixteen-year-old that it is up to him or her to decide about church and Bible study? The parents are washing their hands of the responsibility they accepted on the day they had their child baptized and promised to see to his or her ongoing information and formation in faith.

When we hear a co-worker spreading gossip about another, we can tell ourselves that it is none of our business. That's washing our hands of our responsibility to respect the good name of others.

Anytime we find ourselves washing our hands of our Christian responsibility, we end up handing over another for some type of flogging. While it may not be the same type of beating that was given to Jesus, nevertheless, it leaves others handed over to their enemies.

As you pray this mystery, think about the responsibilities that you have washed away. Be sorrowful for what you have done and/or failed to do.

Option 2

Scripture: "... Pilate, wishing to satisfy the crowd, released Barabbas...; and after flogging Jesus, he handed him over to be crucified." (Mark 15:15)

Sorrowful Mysteries

Reflection: Before a man was crucified, a Roman punishment which had to be administered by Roman soldiers, he was flogged. The whipping with leather whips containing pieces of bone or metal or shell was considered a preparation for crucifixion. It was designed to weaken the condemned so that he would die quickly once he was nailed or tied to the wood of the cross.

In Mark's Gospel, the Roman governor does not order that Jesus be crucified because he is guilty of any crime. Rather, Pilate orders Jesus to be flogged and crucified in order to satisfy the yelling crowd which has been stirred up by the high priests. Pilate attempts to satisfy the crowd by releasing Barabbas, a prisoner who had committed murder during a recent insurrection.

The author of Mark's Gospel is making a pun which is missed unless one knows a little Hebrew. Barabbas means *son of the father*. The guilty *son of the father*, Barabbas, is released from custody while the innocent Jesus, the real Son of the Father, is flogged and condemned to death.

We, too, live in a world where the guilty often go free and the innocent are often flogged and condemned to some kind of death because we wish to satisfy ourselves or a small crowd of people. For example, consider those upon whom we pin blame for something that we did or failed to do. Students often put the blame on their dog, parents, or work for not having their homework done. Co-workers often point fingers at each other for tasks that haven't been completed on time. Congregations often assign fault to their pastors for some project that remains unfinished. The lies, the unkind words, the gossip—all are types of floggings that we give to those others whom we have condemned to death. And while they may satisfy us for a time, sooner or later we recognize what we have done.

As you pray this mystery, reflect on all those you have given over to flogging and death. Be sorrowful for what you have done or failed to do. And remember that all people are sons and daughters of the Father.

Option 3

Scripture: "[Pilate said to the chief priests, the leaders, and the people,] 'You brought me this man as one who was perverting the people, and here I have examined him in your presence and have not found this man guilty of any of your charges against him. I will therefore have him flogged and release him.'" (Luke 23:14, 16)

Reflection: The easiest way to characterize the Lukan Pilate is to say that the governor thinks Jesus is innocent of any crime. In fact, in Luke's Gospel, Pilate three times declares Jesus to be not guilty. After the second and third pronouncements of Jesus' guiltlessness, Pilate declares that he will have Jesus flogged and then release him. However, Luke never records that Pilate scourged him before, finally, handing him over to crucifixion.

Luke's account of Jesus' passion is unique. Not only does Pilate three times declare Jesus innocent of any accusations, but Herod, who makes a cameo appearance in Luke's Gospel, also finds him faultless. One of the criminals, who get speaking parts in Luke's Gospel, states that Jesus is innocent. And the centurion at the cross when Jesus dies proclaims that he was blameless.

According to the author of Luke's Gospel, Jesus dies the death of a martyr; he is a witness to all that he has preached and taught throughout the narrative. Jesus has proclaimed God's kingdom and stood firm in his testimony about it. Thus, he is the model of discipleship; those who follow him must witness to the truth even if it means death or martyrdom. In the Acts of the Apostles, Luke's second volume, Stephen is presented as one of the first witnesses to Jesus; his fate is martyrdom through stoning.

In our day and time, we, too, are challenged to be witnesses to our faith no matter what the price. It's easy to be a Christian when no one is threatening us with flogging or crucifixion; it is not so easy when we must stand up for our catholic truth. For example, adhering to the truth that the death penalty should be abolished is not easy to do in a culture of death. Speaking the truth about any research that treats a human being as if he or she were a thing is not easy in a culture that thinks that we should do medically whatever we can do.

As you pray this sorrowful mystery, reflect upon the ways that you are challenged to witness to your faith. Ask God to give you strength to stand firm, even if it means martyrdom.

Option 4

Scripture: "... Pilate took Jesus and had him flogged." (John 19:1)

Reflection: John's Gospel says that Jesus was flogged or scourged or whipped severely. This small detail in John becomes a very long scene in movies featuring Jesus' trial, like *Jesus of Nazareth* (1977), *King of Kings* (1961), *Jesus* (1999), and, especially, *The Passion of the Christ* (2004). Movie-makers often exploit this element with lots of blood flowing out of gaping wounds on Jesus' back.

The author of John's Gospel gives no details of the scourging; he doesn't even mention how it was accomplished. Based on what was common practice in the first century, a prisoner could have his clothes pulled off and his hands tied around a pillar or post. Then a man wielding a single whip or one with several leather strips with lead beads or shells attached to the ends proceeded to beat the prisoner with a set number of lashes in order to prepare him for death.

Forms of beating have existed through history. The "rule of thumb" in England originally referred to the size of the stick a husband could use to beat his wife; it could be no larger than his thumb. Today, we'd call it spouse abuse. In schools children were beaten often with rulers, yard sticks, paddles, or spanked. Often called "the board of education," the instrument was used to discipline unruly students. Today, we'd call it child abuse. Slaves who failed to live up to their master's expectations or who ran way were often tied to a post and whipped by their owner. And those who failed to complete an order or deserted any branch of the armed forces were often flogged by their commanding officer.

Such treatment repulses us today, but it goes on nevertheless. It may not be a physical flogging that leaves whelps or wounds, but a verbal lashing by a spouse, teacher, or parent can hurt psychologically: "I don't love you. I hate you. Get out of my life. You're good for nothing. You're stupid." Such verbal scourging takes longer to heal, if it ever does, and it leaves scars that often last a lifetime.

As you pray this mystery, reflect on the verbal scourging you have given to others, make a promise to discipline your tongue, and, sorrowfully, ask God for help to avoid future tongue lashings.

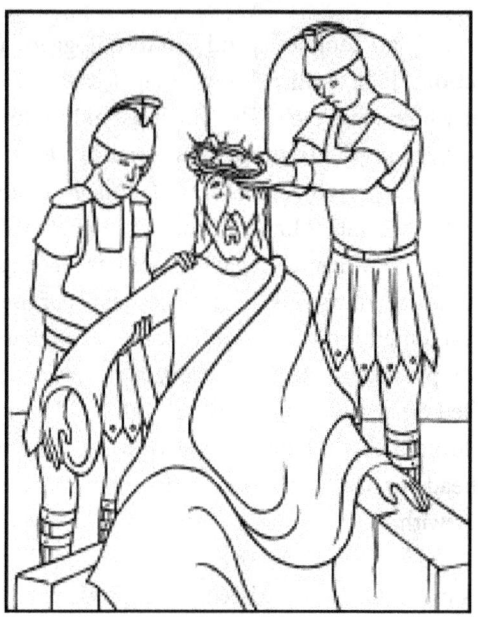

The Crowning with Thorns

Celebrated: Palm Sunday of the Passion of the Lord and Friday of the Passion of the Lord (Good Friday)

Option 1

Scripture: "[The soldiers] stripped [Jesus] and put a scarlet robe on him, and after twisting some thorns into a crown, they put it on his head. They put a reed in his right hand and knelt before him and mocked him, saying, 'Hail, King of the Jews!'" (Matt 27:28)

Sorrowful Mysteries

Reflection: The author of Matthew's Gospel states that the Roman soldiers put a scarlet robe on Jesus along with the crown of thorns. Obviously, they use one of their red Roman cloaks along with the thorny crown to declare that Jesus is not only King of the Jews, but also King of the Gentiles. With the reed/scepter in his right hand and the Roman soldiers kneeling before him, there can be no doubt that Jesus rules the whole world. The truth shines through the grotesqueness of the scene and compliments a Matthean theme woven throughout the book.

Matthew's Gospel portrays Jesus identifying himself with the unusual: the hungry, the thirsty, the stranger, the naked, the sick, the imprisoned, the prostitute, and, most importantly, the Gentiles. Those who do the right thing for the least of people do it to him.

The outcasts of Jesus' day continue to exist in our own day. We may even find ourselves looking down our noses at the social outcasts. When we see a bag lady or a homeless man, do we think first of the injustice of their situations, or do we wonder what each did to end up in the condition he or she is in? It is difficult for those of us who live in good homes or apartments to identify with family members who got tossed out on the street because they could not pay their rent or utility bills after losing a job that went to another country. We can find what we may consider other grotesque figures dressed in black sporting blue or red hair in school, in underpaid hotel cleaning staff who speak a language that is not ours, in any people who wear a different color of skin than we do.

Jesus is King of all those people, including us. He chose not to sit in a big chair on a throne dressed in royal red with a golden crown glittering on his head and a silver scepter in his right hand. Jesus reigns as king from the cross, bearing only a crown of thorns on his head.

So, as you pray this mystery, name for yourself those you think of as outsiders. Be sorrowful that we continue to separate what Jesus attempted to unite through his own kingship.

Option 2

Scripture: ". . . [The soldiers] clothed [Jesus] in a purple cloak; and after twisting some thorns into a crown, they put it on him." (Mark 15:17)

Reflection: We have a tendency to focus on the thorns in this mystery. Many Good Friday crosses display wreaths of thorny rose-bush branches or large needles from a wild thorn tree. We would do better to look at the crown and the cloak accompanying it. Mark's Gospel says that the Roman soldiers dress Jesus in a crown of thorns and a purple cloak.

The author of Mark's Gospel portrays truth emerging from irony. Jesus is crowned king and hailed as such by the Roman occupation forces of Palestine. He is dressed in royal purple. His crown depicts him as an emperor, since Roman emperors are often depicted on coins and reliefs wearing a laurel wreath crown of victory. With a reed for a scepter and the soldiers declaring, "Hail, King of the Jews"—echoing the "Hail, Caesar!" of the ancient Romans—the truth in the irony of Jesus' kingship is complete.

Jesus rules from a position of powerlessness, and that is what gives him his kingship. Emperors and kings rule by power and lineage, but Jesus reigns as servant. He is not interested in control or manipulation of others. His ministry is one of care for others. So, he is ironically crowned by the very forces responsible for his death! And Jesus wields his powerless kingship to set free all who are oppressed, even the oppressors.

Some people create their crowns out of the success of trampling over others to get ahead. Others fashion crowns through the control they exert with language that provokes feelings of guilt and remorse. Through their manipulation of others, some weave a crown of poor choices with horrible consequences. Other form crowns by visiting the sick, holding the hands of the dying, tutoring students, raising other people's kids, being a good neighbor, and ministering in one's church. Looking carefully, we see that they can be either invisible crowns of thorns or crowns of service.

As you pray this sorrowful mystery of Jesus being crowned with thorns, reflect on how your crown is one of thorns or one of powerless service to others.

Option 3

Scripture: "... The soldiers wove a crown of thorns and put it on [Jesus'] head, and they dressed him in a purple robe. They kept coming up to him, saying, 'Hail, King of the Jews!' and striking him on the face." (John 19:2–4)

Reflection: The author of John's Gospel has relocated the story of Jesus being flogged, crowned with thorns, dressed in royal purple, and mocked as king to the middle of the trial with Pilate. Mark, who dressed Jesus in royal purple, and Matthew, who dressed Jesus in Roman red, place the crowning with thorns scene immediately before the narrative of Jesus being led off to crucifixion. Luke contains no story about Jesus being dressed in any color nor one about him wearing a thorny crown.

John places the crown of thorns scene and portrays Jesus dressed in royal purple in the middle of the secular trial scene before Pilate because he wants to present Jesus as king. Pilate asks Jesus about his kingship, and Jesus acknowledges that he has come into the world as a king to testify to the truth. After he is crowned and robed in purple, Pilate brings Jesus out of the barracks and presents him to the people. "Here is the man," he says (John 19:5b). Then, after taking Jesus inside his headquarters, the two of them dialogue about power. Jesus makes it clear that even Pilate's power comes from God. As the narrative unfolds, clearly it becomes a contest between two kings: Jesus and the emperor, who at that time was Tiberius.

Often the religious king finds himself set against the secular king. While we in the United States pride ourselves on the separation of church and state, even in such a duplicitous arrangement often they come head to head. Do we follow the religious truth that killing is wrong, or do we permit whatever killing the state deems acceptable? Do we follow the religious truth that honesty is the best policy, or do we allow a coloring of the truth to protect the guilty?

Our church teaches us the sacredness of Sunday, while our culture puts it as part of the weekend for golf, tennis, shopping, and other activities that have nothing to do with keeping the day holy.

As you pray this mystery, reflect upon your own duplicity. Notice which things you name fit under the "Jesus is King" category and which fit under the "State is King" category. Be sorrowful if you discover that Jesus is not king over your whole life. Remember that following the profane is often a strike on the face of your religion.

Option 4

Scripture: "Then I saw heaven opened, and there was a white horse! Its rider is called Faithful and True. . . . His eyes are like a flame of fire, and on his head are many diadems . . . . He is clothed in a robe dipped in blood, and his name is called The Word of God. On his robe and on his thigh he has a name inscribed, 'King of kings and Lord of lords.'" (Rev 19:11–13, 16)

Reflection: The Book of Revelation presents Christ as the universal judge of the world. His appearance is an epiphany (white horse). His name is Faithful, meaning that he trusted God all the way through death. His name is also True, meaning loyal. His knowledge is infinite (eyes) and his diadems or crowns display him as king; the crown of thorns in the gospels has been traded in for a crown of victory in the Book of Revelation. His blood-dipped robe recalls his scourging and thorny crown and death on a cross. Christ is indeed the King of kings and Lord of lords. He is the Lamb who was slain and now lives forever.

Within so much exaltation, it may be hard to pray a sorrowful mystery. But the exalted Christ, as the Book of Revelation makes clear, was first the suffering Jesus. Because of his faithfulness and loyalty to God with his crown of thorns all the way to the cross, the Lamb, who once was slain, has been raised from the dead and designated king of the universe. In other words, Good Friday always precedes Easter Sunday.

That is a fact worth remembering, especially in a culture that often takes its comfortable way of life too seriously. Modern medicine means that we live longer and longer. Modern attitudes toward death mean that it is so far removed from us that we no longer know how to walk with another through death. Modern conveniences mean that we do less and less. Fast food means that many of us don't even know how to cook. So, as a culture we can easily bask in the comfortableness of Easter and forget about the crowned suffering of Good Friday.

Good Friday depicts the uncomfortableness of suffering and death. It reminds us that sacrifice is still a part of a well-lived life. The new Passover Lamb, Christ, had first to be slain before God raised him from the dead.

As you pray this mystery, reflect upon the ways that you have gotten too comfortable with your faith. In your sorrow, ask God to crown you with uncomfortableness so that you can plumb the truth of this mystery.

The Carrying of the Cross

Celebrated: Palm Sunday of the Passion of the Lord and Friday of the Passion of the Lord (Good Friday)

Option 1

Scripture: "As [the soldiers] went out, they came upon a man from Cyrene named Simon; they compelled this man to carry [Jesus'] cross." (Matt 27:32)

Reflection: The author of Matthew's Gospel, who used Mark's Gospel as one of his sources, omits the naming of the sons of Simon of Cyrene because his readers would not have know them. He does follow Mark's story about the Roman soldiers compelling Simon to carry Jesus' cross; no details are given as to where or why that occurred.

Whoever carried Jesus' cross probably hauled only the crossbeam to the place of crucifixion. The upright post stayed in place and the crossbeam fitted over it. While it was customary for a condemned man to carry his own crossbeam in order to further humiliate him and turn the capital punishment event into a public spectacle in order to intimidate others, those weakened by scourging, hunger, or dehydration often needed assistance

Matthew, like Mark before him, is not interested in explaining how Jesus and his cross got to the place of crucifixion, but, rather, wants to teach discipleship. He wants to give the reader an understanding of what it means to follow Jesus. Matthew does not paint a pretty picture of discipleship, especially insofar as it entails denying self, taking the cross, following Jesus, and enduring persecution. But that was the reality of the last third of the first century CE for those first disciples of Jesus of Nazareth. While we might prefer crosses with wheels on them today, many discovered death because they were followers of Jesus.

In some countries, Christians are still persecuted. But in most of the world crosses are few and far between. Diseases, like cancer and AIDS, are crosses. Those in automobile, plane, train, climbing, and swimming accidents may carry the cross of healing and/or irreparable damage of some kind. Trauma, abuse, and the unwillingness to forgive can be counted among the psychological crosses some people tote. The emotional strains of marriage and child-rearing are crosses parents carry. No matter what the burden, the focus must be on discipleship. The question is always this: How well do we carry our crosses throughout the living of our lives?

As you pray this sorrowful mystery, reflect on both the crosses you have carried and those you now carry and how those illustrate your understanding of discipleship.

Option 2

Scripture: "[The soldiers] compelled a passer-by, who was coming in from the country, to carry [Jesus'] cross; it was Simon of Cyrene, the father of Alexander and Rufus." (Mark 15:21)

Reflection: In movies about Jesus, he is usually portrayed as struggling to carry his cross to the hill of crucifixion. Most of the time Jesus is seen carrying a cross formed from two heavy beams of timber that resemble railroad ties. However, the author of Mark's Gospel portrays Simon of Cyrene carrying Jesus' cross; that would not have been the two planks already nailed together, but only the crossbeam. Usually, the Romans left the one timber in place and put the notched crossbeam on top of it.

Mark notes that Simon came from North Africa—Cyrene. He would have been in Jerusalem as a pilgrim for Passover, or he could have migrated there. His coming in from the country refers to his passage from outside to inside the city walls. Furthermore, he must have been known by Mark's readers, since the author names him as the father of Alexander and Rufus.

Simon of Cyrene is forced to carry Jesus' crossbeam. In Mark's Gospel, Simon is forced into the role of a disciple because all the disciples have run away in fear. Judas betrayed Jesus. Peter denied knowing him. Even an unnamed young man dressed in a white sheet ran away naked when Jesus was arrested. Jesus is abandoned by every one—except for Simon of Cyrene.

We, too, may feel or think that we have been abandoned by everyone, but some Simon suddenly appears. People who experience depression often think that they are all alone in the world, until a doctor or therapist helps them carry their crosses. Those who have cancer can feel abandoned to their disease unless the nurse administering chemotherapy treatments helps them carry their crosses. Even good friends can experience abandonment until a Simon comes along to help them restore their relationship.

As you pray this sorrowful mystery, reflect upon your own experiences of abandonment, and name the Simon of Cyrene who helped you carry your cross.

Option 3

Scripture: "As [the soldiers] led [Jesus] away, they seized a man, Simon of Cyrene, who was coming from the country, and they laid the cross on him, and made him carry it behind Jesus." (Luke 23:26)

Reflection: The author of Luke's Gospel is very careful to note that Simon of Cyrene carries Jesus' cross while walking behind Jesus. Discipleship in Luke's Gospel is following, walking behind, Jesus and bearing witness to the truth as he did. Earlier in the gospel, the Lukan Jesus makes it very clear that anyone who wants to be his follower must take up the cross daily and follow him. Simon of Cyrene represents the authentic disciple who daily picks up the cross and treads in Jesus' footsteps—even though he is forced into doing so.

If we think about it, we, too, are often forced into carrying a cross we would not voluntarily pick up. For example, parishioners can be pushed by their pastor to accept a seat on a committee; they wouldn't volunteer to serve on the committee. But, as everyone sooner or later discovers, committee work often entails bearing lots of crosses—working with other members, listening to fellow parishioners' complaints, meeting the expectations of the pastor, etc.

No one volunteers to carry some medical crosses, like cancer, major surgery, high blood pressure, high cholesterol, etc. No one volunteers to bear psychological crosses, like depression, anger, stress, etc. And no one volunteers to haul emotional crosses, like divorce, run-away children, abusive spouses, etc.

While we don't want to glorify such crosses, we also don't want to ignore Simon, who, once he was compelled, carried Jesus' cross and was, hopefully, a better man because of it. If we take some time

Sorrowful Mysteries

to reflect upon the crosses we have been forced to bear—those for which we did not volunteer—we may discover that we became disciples without even being aware of it. We walked behind Jesus, daily dragging our crosses, and we have been changed because of it.

As you reflect upon this sorrowful mystery, think about the crosses you have been forced to carry and the discipleship that ensued from each of them. Be thankful that God has helped you daily to take up the cross and follow behind Jesus.

Option 4

Scripture: ". . . [C]arrying the cross by himself, [Jesus] went out to what is called The Place of the Skull, which in Hebrew is called Golgotha." (John 19:17)

Reflection: The authors of Mark's Gospel and Matthew's Gospel make it clear that Simon of Cyrene carries Jesus' crossbeam. The author of Luke's Gospel is more specific, indicating that Simon carries the crossbeam behind Jesus. Only John's Gospel portrays Jesus as carrying his cross alone.

The author of John's Gospel narrates the scene that way in order to show that Jesus is in charge of his own fate, even to his last breath. From the very opening of John's Gospel the reader is told that Jesus is the incarnate Word of God. Jesus is God. Often he says, "I AM," a reference to the name the Holy One gives Moses at the burning bush scene in the Hebrew Bible (Old Testament) Book of Exodus. Because Jesus is God, he needs no help completing his work.

In John's Gospel, Jesus' carrying his cross is merely a step towards his glorification. Previously, he had prayed to the Heavenly Father, asking him to glorify the Son so that the Son might glorify him. He stated that God had given him authority over all people to give them eternal life. The finishing of his work on earth—his crucifixion, death, and resurrection—glorifies the Mighty One, who, in turn, gives the Son the glory he had in God's presence before the world existed.

As we carry some of our crosses alone, we can be tempted to fall prey to the "pity me" point of view. The portrayal of Jesus carrying the cross alone in John's Gospel serves as a corrective to that mentality. We carry some crosses alone because they praise God. We carry some crosses alone because they bring us one step closer to eternal life.

We may have to carry the cross of a single parent alone. Minimum wages may be another cross we have to bear alone. Repair of a relationship may require that we carry the cross alone to the other person. And, of course, almost all medical treatment means that we carry the cross all by ourselves.

As you pray this sorrowful mystery, name the crosses you have carried alone, and reflect upon how each has brought you one step closer to eternal life or glorification.

The Crucifixion

Celebrated: Palm Sunday of the Passion of the Lord and Friday of the Passion of the Lord (Good Friday)

Sorrowful Mysteries

Option 1

Scripture: "... [W]hen [the soldiers] had crucified [Jesus], they divided his clothes among themselves by casting lots...." (Matt 27:35)

Reflection: The Romans often followed a master plan when designing a new city. One main street would run north and south and the other one would bisect it east and west. Thus, the city would be divided into four quadrants, forming what the Romans thought of as order. The two main streets bisecting each other formed a cross. Anyone who caused disorder, such as murderers and traitors, were put to death on the instrument representing order. Those who caused chaos in the orderly city were crucified, and their crucifixion served as a deterrent for anyone thinking of disturbing the *pax Romana*, the peace of Rome.

The author of Matthew's Gospel does not describe crucifixion, because his readers knew about the variety of ways it was done. Seldom did the Romans put to death a single criminal; they preferred a large group of men so as to make a bigger public spectacle. After striping the prisoner naked in order to shame him as much as possible, nails were usually driven through his wrists—not hands—and feet. He may or may not also be tired at the arms to the crossbeam for support, and a small wooden footrest might be nailed below his feet to give him leverage. The goal of crucifixion was not to kill the criminal quickly, but to prolong his suffering as long as possible. Some of the crucified hung alive on their crosses for days, exposed to the elements and wild animals, before finally succumbing to asphyxiation.

Today, we have found other ways to crucify people. A firing squad or the electric chair may still be used in some places, but a lethal injection is more sterile and causes less of a spectacle with viewers seated behind a window in a theater-like room. Besides such deadly crucifixions there are the non-deadly ones each of us manages to impose on others. For example, we refuse to relinquish the old image of a person as an alcoholic, drug abuser, or street person no matter how much he or she has changed. In national, state, local, office, and home politics, leaders crucify each other on economic, war, domestic, and foreign policy issue. Our ways of crucifying may be more humane, but the result is the same: the denigration of a human being at his or her expense.

As you pray this mystery, reflect on the crucifixions in which you have taken part and sorrowfully ask God for forgiveness.

Option 2

Scripture: "[The soldiers] crucified [Jesus], and divided his clothes among them, casting lots to decide what each should take." (Mark 15:24)

Reflection: The author of Mark's Gospel describes crucifixion both briefly and starkly. He is brief insofar as all he writes that the Roman soldiers crucified Jesus after offering him the narcotic of wine mixed with myrrh, which he didn't take. Mark does not provide any details concerning the method of crucifixion; from history we know that the Romans employed several forms, such as nailing the criminal to the crossbeam through his wrists and, once the crossbeam was fitted over the standing upright, nailing his feet to it through the ankles. Sometimes a criminal could have been tied with ropes to the cross to lengthen his time of suffering. History even provides types of crosses other than the "T" described above, such as the ones in the forms of a "†" and an "X".

The author of Mark's Gospel is also stark insofar as he writes about the soldiers casting lots to decide what each should have of Jesus' clothes. The condemned man would have few clothes, probably an outer garment, some type of underwear, and maybe sandals, but those were valuable in the ancient world, and a soldier, especially one on execution duty whose pay was minimal, could sell whatever he won in the lottery to increase his basic wage. The casting of lots involved each soldier putting a small stone with his mark on it in a cup. One would shake the cup, and the first stone to fall out would be the winner.

Contrary to popular depiction, the criminal would have been crucified naked. Crucifixion was considered to be one of the most horrendous forms of capital punishment. Its purpose was not only to kill the criminal, but to embarrass him as much as possible and shame him as much as possible before he died. Mark's minimal description of the crucifixion yields maximum results.

As you pray this sorrowful mystery, reflect upon the things that you consider minimal in your life and how maximum they might really be. By contemplating the little events of our lives we may find God working through them quietly, but, nevertheless, powerfully.

Option 3

Scripture: "Two others also, who were criminals, were led away to be put to death with [Jesus]. When they came to the place that is called The Skull, [the soldiers] crucified Jesus there with the criminals, one on his right and one on his left." (Luke 23:32–33)

Reflection: While both the author of Mark's Gospel and the author of Matthew's Gospel mention the two criminals co-crucified with Jesus, only the author of Luke's Gospel takes special notice of them and gives them speaking parts. Each of the criminals serves an important purpose in Luke's narrative.

One criminal aligns himself with the Jewish leadership in deriding Jesus. He taunts Jesus by implying that if he were the Messiah, he would save himself and both criminals. This criminal represents those who refuse to repent.

The other criminal takes the opposite stance. He acknowledges that he is guilty of his crime and deserves to be put to death. Thus, he repents, and he asks Jesus to remember him when Jesus gets into his kingdom.

Repentance is an important theme running through Luke's Gospel and his second volume, the Acts of the Apostles. Repentance means to change one's mind about something. In this case, the criminal changes his mind about his innocence and proclaims his guilt. Once a change in mind has occurred, then a change in behavior follows. In this case, the criminal doesn't ask to be saved but to be remembered by Jesus, who promises him Paradise.

Jesus can only save those who repent. That's the message woven through Luke's two volumes. If seeing the innocent Savior of the world nailed to two pieces of wood can spark repentance in a criminal, what more should it kindle in those who profess to be his followers?

Repentance is not just saying that one is sorry for what one has done. In Lukan understanding, repentance implies change in one's thinking which causes change in one's behavior. For example, once you decide that you are addicted to alcohol, drugs, food, or sex, you change your mind about drinking too much alcohol, taking too many drugs, eating too much food, or engaging in excessive sexual activity. Once the change in mind is in process, then the change in behavior follows in terms of no more drinking, no more drugs, controlled eating, and only married sex.

As you pray this sorrowful mystery, reflect upon what you have repented and of what you may need to repent.

Option 4

Scripture: "At The Place of the Skull] they crucified [Jesus], and with him two others, one on either side, with Jesus between them. Pilate also had an inscription written and put on the cross. It read, 'Jesus of Nazareth, the King of the Jews.' . . . It was written in Hebrew, in Latin, and in Greek." (John 19:18–20)

Reflection: Unique to John's Gospel is the inscription ordered by Pilate to be placed on the cross: Jesus of Nazareth, the King of the Jews. It is familiar to catholics because it appears on most crucifixes in churches in its Latin abbreviation, I.N.R.I. (*Iesus Nazarenus Rex Iudaeorum*). The author of Mark's Gospel states that the sign reads "The King of the Jews"; Matthew writes that the placard declares "This is Jesus, the King of the Jews"; and Luke puts "This is the King of the Jews" on the cross.

By declaring that the inscription was written in Hebrew, Latin, and Greek, the author of John's Gospel emphasizes the public and universal character of Jesus' mission. Hebrew, Latin, and Greek were the three languages of the Roman Empire. Jews could read Hebrew; Romans could read Latin, and Greeks could read Greek. Thus, Jesus is crucified for the whole world according to John.

The word *catholic* means *universal*. A catholic is a member of the universal church. That's why a catholic from Chicago can participate in Mass in Rome, Paris, and New York. It is the same church spread throughout the world; the local gathering is just that: a manifestation of the universal church. This understanding is in contrast to Protestantism's congregationalism, that is, one belongs to a specific congregation and not to the universal church. While many catholics are Roman, there are other types of catholics, such as Eastern Rite, Anglican, etc.

The Johannine Jesus makes clear that the purpose of his crucifixion is to draw all people to himself. He came into the world to drive out the ruler of the world and to be lifted up on the cross for all. Such universality can be easily overlooked in our sometimes narrow approach to faith. We can be so focused on the parish that we forget that it is a miniature of the whole church. So, as you pray this sorrowful mystery, reflect upon the worldwide mission that you have had as a member of the catholic church.

4

The Glorious Mysteries

The Resurrection

The Ascension

The Descent of the Holy Spirit Upon the Apostles

The Assumption

The Coronation of Mary

The Glorious Mysteries

The Resurrection

Celebrated: The Easter Vigil in the Holy Night and Easter Sunday of the Resurrection of the Lord

Option 1

Scripture: "After the sabbath, as the first day of the week was dawning, Mary Magdalene and the other Mary went to see the tomb. And suddenly there was a great earthquake; for an angel of the Lord, descending from heaven, came and rolled back the stone and sat on it." (Matt 28:1–2)

Reflection: The author of Matthew's Gospel has a flair for apocalyptic details. As soon as Jesus dies in the Matthean narrative, there is an earthquake that causes tombs to open and the resurrection of the dead to occur. The effect of Jesus' death, according to Matthew, is immediate resurrection for the saints who had fallen asleep. In other words, Jesus' death is a theophany, a manifestation of God.

It will come as no surprise, then, that Matthew adds the apocalyptic drama of an earthquake to his resurrection story, too. Two women watch an angel roll back the tomb's entry stone and sit upon it. The guards placed there by the Jewish authorities almost die of fright. The angel of the Lord proclaims that the tomb is empty, that Jesus has been raised from the dead. A theophany has occurred. There is no body in the tomb. Matthew is dealing with an old rumor that someone stole Jesus' body and then declared him raised. By portraying the guards at the tomb and the angel opening it, Matthew thinks he has dispelled that rumor.

Not being sure as to how describe resurrection, Matthew later adds that the women see Jesus and take hold of his feet. Likewise, Jesus meets the eleven disciples in Galilee and sends them on a mission of making disciples, baptizing, and teaching; he promises to be with them until the end of the world.

For Matthew, resurrection, probably best described as a bodiless body, means that God guarantees life for the righteous through death. Throughout Matthew's Gospel, Jesus teaches a higher righteousness, usually understood as doing the right thing because it is the right thing to do. A person goes beyond the minimum set by the Torah or Law in order to be holy or to act like God. Just as God does not choose favorites, but loves all people equally, so are followers of Jesus challenged to love all people. Their broader ability to love makes them righteous and means that they will always do the right thing—even if it means death—because they trust that God will raise them from the dead.

As you pray this glorious mystery, reflect upon the apocalyptic and theophanic moments in your life, those times when God sent an earthquake your way to enable you to see what the right thing to do was and you did it.

Option 2

Scripture: ". . . [V]ery early on the first day of the week, when the sun had risen, [Mary Magdalene and Mary the Mother of James, and Salome] went to the tomb. . . . When they looked up, they saw that the stone, which was very large, had . . . been rolled back." (Mark 16:2, 4)

Reflection: Strictly speaking, there are no eye-witness accounts of Christ's resurrection in the Christian Bible (New Testament), because resurrection is a statement of faith that cannot be proved. Mark's Gospel says that three women found the tomb's stone rolled away and a young man seated on the right side of the place where Jesus' body had been placed.

The empty tomb is a metaphor for resurrection, but the empty tomb does not prove resurrection. If you were walking through a cemetery and saw an opening, you would reach one of the following conclusions: (1) someone was going to be buried there, (2) someone had robbed a grave, or (3) someone had been exhumed. You would not conclude that someone had been raised from the dead!

We don't know what resurrection from the dead means because it is on the other side of death, and we have no knowledge of what is over there. That is why it is easier to explain resurrection by saying that it is not resuscitation, but it is like an empty tomb.

The author of Mark's Gospel believes that God raised Jesus from the dead. For Mark, resurrection means that God does not abandon faithful people in death even when they may think such is the case. Mark attempts to make clear that resurrection is the "something more" that we experience throughout our lives.

While loving and raising children, parents often say that there must be something more; they discover it in their adult children and grandchildren. Teachers in schools discover it in their former students who thank them for something the instructor has long forgotten. After a long day, white, blue, and no collar workers discover the something more when they are told that they did a good job. That "something more" to life is a glimpse of resurrection.

As you pray this mystery, recall some of your own glorious resurrection experiences of something more.

Option 3

Scripture: ". . . On the first day of the week, at early dawn, [the women] came to the tomb, taking the spices that they had prepared. They found the stone rolled away from the tomb, but when they went in, they did not find the body." (Luke 24:1–3)

Reflection: The author of Luke's Gospel portrays spice-bearing women finding the open tomb without a body inside. Two men in dazzling clothes appear to the women; they remind them of the words Jesus had spoken about his handing over, crucifixion, and resurrection. After remembering Jesus' words, they go to the eleven disciples and proclaim what they have seen, but the eleven discount their words as idle chatter. Peter goes to the tomb but is only amazed by what he sees. The author then proceeds to narrate the walk-to-Emmaus story and Jesus' appearance to his disciples in Jerusalem before he ascends to heaven on Easter Sunday evening.

Luke conceptualizes resurrection as a bodiless body that can appear and disappear. The resurrected Christ appears and disappears quickly after breaking bread with the two travelers once they have reached Emmaus. He appears to his disciples in Jerusalem and eats cooked fish in their presence. Then, he leads them to Bethany and disappears into the heavens.

For the author of Luke's Gospel discipleship involves witnessing suffering and death before resurrection. Repeatedly, Jesus teaches that those who are his followers are willing to embrace suffering and death daily in the hope of new life afterward. In other words, resurrection always follows suffering and death.

We live in a culture that doesn't like suffering and death. In fact we will do anything and everything to avoid either. This is not to imply that we should be masochists in our suffering. It is to imply that we have become experts at avoiding one of the very things that makes us human and shapes our character. Lots of energy is spent trying to find a way around suffering and death rather than walking through it to the new life on the other side. Lies enable one to avoid the consequences of telling the truth, but deprive him or her of the integrity of new life.

As you pray this glorious mystery, think about the sufferings and deaths you have endured and how they have made you a better person, one filled with new life.

Option 4

Scripture: "Early on the first day of the week, while it was still dark, Mary Magdalene came to the tomb and saw that the stone had been removed from the tomb. So she ran and went to Simon Peter and the other disciple, the one whom Jesus loved, and said to them, 'They have taken the Lord out of the tomb, and we do not know where they have laid him.'" (John 20:1–2)

Reflection: The author of John's Gospel shares a tradition quite different from that of Mark, Matthew, and Luke when it comes to narrating the empty tomb. Mary Magdalene is the star of John's story. Once she runs to Simon Peter and the unnamed beloved disciple and tells them what she has discovered, they race to the tomb and examine it carefully. John is careful to point out that the beloved disciple sees and believes, which, of course, is a theme that is woven throughout the Fourth Gospel.

So, for the author John's Gospel, resurrection means that seeing Jesus' bodiless body is believing—but not always. Peter sees the empty tomb, but John does not tell us that he believes. The beloved disciple sees and believes. Mary Magdalene sees and believes. The disciples see and believe. And, after Jesus appears to Thomas, he sees and believes.

But the author realizes that he has to put a stop to the scenario of seeing and believing. Otherwise, no one after the first believers will ever believe unless they see the risen Christ. So, the Johannine Jesus pronounces a beatitude about those who have not seen and yet have come to believe before the author states that he has written his book so that the reader may read and believe that Jesus is the Messiah, the Son of God. Later, another writer added another chapter to John's Gospel, often labeled "Epilogue," which necessitated a second ending to the Fourth Gospel.

Do we, like Mary Magdalene, the beloved disciple, the other disciples, and Thomas, have to see in order to believe? Or, is our trust of God strong enough for us to travel throughout our lives without ever needing a sign to confirm our faith? Obviously, in the way John narrates the story, he thinks that the higher calling is not seeing and yet believing, but he also writes a whole book about those who have to see in order to believe!

As you pray this glorious mystery, reflect upon your own faith in Jesus as the Messiah and Son of God and determine if you believe because you see or if you believe despite not seeing.

The Ascension

Celebrated: Forty Days after Easter Sunday or the Seventh Sunday of Easter, The Ascension of the Lord

The Glorious Mysteries

Option 1

Scripture: ". . . [T]hen the Lord Jesus, after he had spoken to [the eleven], was taken up into heaven and sat down at the right hand of God." (Mark 16:19)

Reflection: At first glance, the account of the Ascension of Jesus in Mark's Gospel might be determined as nothing other than the usual narration of the rocket-ship-like-Jesus blasting off into the heavens to take his seat on the right side of God. However, after reading Mark's Gospel more carefully, the astute reader would notice that the ascension is part of the longer ending of the oldest gospel. In fact, Mark's Gospel ends three times! There is the original ending at 16:8, the shorter ending (also part of 16:8), and the longer ending at 16:9–20.

No one disputes the fact that Mark's Gospel has three endings and that the shorter and longer endings were added to the original by different authors at various stages in the transmission of the manuscript. The author of Mark's Gospel could never have written an account of the ascension because such display of Jesus' power would reverse the theme of powerlessness he had established in the second half of the story. That's why Mark's empty tomb story ends with the women running away from the tomb and saying nothing to anyone. The gospel ends on a note of powerlessness.

The shorter and longer endings betray the fact that their authors had read Matthew's Gospel and Luke's Gospel. Those additional endings form a summary of the endings of the two narratives that used Mark's Gospel as their primary sources. Thus, a little reverse borrowing is noted here by scribes who considered the original ending of Mark inadequate.

And maybe that is where the truth is to be found in Mark's ascension addition. Our lives as followers of a Jesus, who taught the path of powerlessness, are always inadequate. We find ourselves in positions of power, having to exercise power over others, enjoying the attention of power, etc. None of us enjoys being powerless, but that's what the Markan Jesus taught, and that's how he died.

As you pray this glorious mystery, reflect upon the powerless moments in your life when you were more like the Markan Jesus.

Option 2

Scripture: "While [Jesus] was blessing [his disciples], he withdrew from them and was carried up into heaven." (Luke 24:51)

Reflection: In Luke's Gospel, the risen Jesus makes several post-resurrection appearances on Easter Sunday before he ascends from Bethany that same evening. The author brings to a close the unique mission discussed by Jesus with Moses and Elijah during his transfiguration, namely, his departure—exodus—he was going to accomplish in Jerusalem. So, after arriving in Jerusalem, suffering, dying, and being raised from the dead, the Lukan Jesus completes his mission by leading his disciples to Bethany and departing—"exodusing"—from them, like Elijah, who ascended into heaven in a fiery chariot.

Luke's focus at the end of the gospel is on Jesus' finishing his mission of saving the world. In the annunciation story, Gabriel announces that Mary's child will be called the Son of the Most High; he will inherit David's throne; his kingdom will have no end. Then, from 9:51 Jesus sets his face toward Jerusalem, from where he will be taken up. Having arrived in Jerusalem ten chapters later at 19:29, he makes his triumphant entrance into the city only later to weep over it because those living there do not recognize the kingdom he has established through his teaching and preaching.

We share in Jesus' mission of saving the world through the way we live our lives. When people practice religion, it often becomes something to do only on Sunday—or even only on Saturday evening. However, for those who believe the mission permeates the fiber of their being. Every word they speak is colored by the gospel. Every act they do or don't do is directed by the teaching of Jesus. Thus, they own the mission that Jesus owned, and in each one's small way he or she furthers the establishment of the kingdom of God.

As you pray this glorious mystery, think about your participation in the mission of Jesus. Is it perfunctory, or has it gotten under your skin and into your soul so that you speak and live it? At the completion of your life, that moment when you take your last breath, when you are ready to make your exodus out of this world, what aspects of Jesus' mission will you have furthered the most?

Option 3

Scripture: "After his suffering [Jesus] presented himself alive to [the apostles] by many convincing proofs, appearing to them during forty days and speaking about the kingdom of God. . . . [A]s they were watching, he was lifted up, and a cloud took him out of their sight. (Acts 1:3, 9)

Reflection: In the Acts of the Apostles, Luke's second volume, the risen Christ appears to his apostles during forty days before he is lifted up from Mount Olivet. Obviously, Luke narrates the ascension in two different ways: the one in the gospel occurring on Easter Sunday evening, and the one in the Acts occurring forty days later.

In the Acts scenario, the author has two purposes: (1) to remove the risen Jesus from the story and (2) to narrate the mission to Jews and Gentiles. In other words, the risen Jesus has to disappear for the mission to be enacted according to the Lukan theological schema. If he remains, then he, instead of the apostles, would be entrusted with the mission of spreading the Good News to the ends of the world.

For Luke, ascension in Acts is nothing other than resurrection in disguise. The same two men in dazzling clothes appear to the women at the tomb and to the apostles after the ascension. In either scenario, the two men announce a vision. They challenge their hearers to open wide their eyes, to see the big picture, to get out of their little box of reality, and to look at the world and its universes from God's perspective. In effect, that is the challenge of the mission—witnessing to God's work throughout the world.

Those who have suffered through such diseases as cancer or undergone transplant surgery often communicate a deeper appreciation for life and death; their vision has been enlarged. When we are open consciously to the multitude of possibilities of living, we may experience ourselves being lifted above the dailyness of existence to see today as just one tiny, disappearing speck on the edge of the horizon. Travel to foreign countries often leaves the pilgrim with alternate ways of believing. Any time of change in our lives enables us to ascend, to get ourselves out of our little picture, and to embrace the big mission of being sent into the world to make it aware of the presence of God.

As you pray this mystery, reflect on your own glorious ascension experiences and thank God for sending you on mission.

Option 4

Scripture: "... [T]he righteousness that comes from faith says, 'Do not say in your heart, "Who will ascend into heaven?"' (that is, to bring Christ down) "or 'Who will descend into the abyss?'" (that is, to bring Christ up from the dead). But what does it say? 'The word is near you, on your lips and in your heart' (that is, the word of faith that we proclaim) ...." (Rom 10:6–8)

Reflection: In Paul's Letter to the Romans, the apostle sets forth his theological position of righteousness by faith. That phrase means that because of what Christ has done, God declares righteous the person who comes to the Holy One in faith. Righteousness is not something that the sinner attains; it is what God has done in Christ.

For Paul, the heights and the depths have been reached by Christ, who came into the world, died, and was raised from the dead. God was in Christ and at work reconciling the world. So, a believer does not need to ascend or to descend in order to earn salvation. Indeed, salvation has already been earned for all by Christ in God. All that a person needs to do is to accept in faith what has already been accomplished and identify himself or herself with the One who achieved it: Christ.

The demonstration that a person has come to righteousness by faith is found in one's behavior. The way one lives in acceptance of God's righteousness shows that he or she has received God's offer of salvation. We are not saved because we do good works, according to Paul—that would be tantamount to earning salvation. We do good works to live the righteousness that God has given to us.

Ascension does not mean leaving the world; in effect, ascension means being more and more immersed in it while living the gracious gift offered to us by God in Christ. Once we confess with our lips and believe in our hearts that God raised Jesus from the dead, we are made righteous by the Holy One. That righteousness spills out of us in our lifestyle of good works. If we look closely, we can see righteousness by faith inscribed in the efforts of those who volunteer to work in soup kitchens, to teach children, to lead youth, to visit the homebound and those in nursing homes, etc. Their good deeds flow out of their faith; they don't volunteer to earn something.

As you pray this glorious mystery, reflect on the works that manifest your righteousness through faith, that is, the ways you immerse your faith into the world.

The Descent of the Holy Spirit Upon the Apostles

Celebrated: Fifty Days after Easter, Pentecost Sunday

Option 1

Scripture: [Jesus said to the eleven and their companions,] ". . . [S]ee, I am sending upon you what my Father promised; so stay here in the city [of Jerusalem] until you have been clothed with power from on high." (Luke 24:49)

Reflection: One way that the author of Luke's Gospel chooses to speak about the Holy Spirit is as the power from on high. That reference at the end his book is meant to echo the reference at the beginning when Gabriel tells Mary that the Holy Spirit will come upon her and the power of the Most High will overshadow her. For Luke, the Holy Spirit is the pure gift of God who guides all people to salvation.

Jesus is conceived by the power of the Holy Spirit; his mother is clothed with the power from on high. After he completes his work on earth and before he takes his last breath, Jesus returns that Spirit to God. Once he is raised from the dead and before he ascends into heaven in Luke's Gospel, Jesus instructs his disciples to wait in Jerusalem for the Father's promised gift that will overshadow them. We have to wait until Luke's second volume, the Acts of the Apostles, for the fulfillment of that promise.

While not as dramatic as Luke likes to describe things, we often are clothed with power from on high, but we are not aware of it. For example, after struggling with an issue for a long time and, finally, reaching a decision, has not some power from on high clothed us in wisdom and enabled us to be content with the direction we have chosen? People preparing for serious surgery can be seen often at peace with their trust placed in the hands of their physicians; they have been clothed with power from on high. Even finding a few right words to say to a grieving friend may indicate that we were filled with the Holy Spirit before we opened our lips

As you pray this mystery, look closely at some of the inconsequential events of your life and determine how you were clothed with power from on high. Thank God for such a glorious gift like the Holy Spirit.

Option 2

Scripture: "When it was evening on that day, the first day of the week, and the doors of the house where the disciples had met were locked . . . , Jesus came and stood among them and . . . breathed on them and said to them, 'Receive the Holy Spirit.'" (John 20:19, 22)

Reflection: Often overlooked in favor of the fiery account of Pentecost in the Acts of the Apostles is the pneumatic account of Pentecost in John's Gospel. The author of the Fourth Gospel portrays Jesus giving the Holy Spirit to his disciples on Easter Sunday evening by breathing on them. The word for breath, wind, and air in Greek, *pneuma*, can also mean *spirit*. So, by breathing on his followers, Jesus is giving them the invisible zephyr of eternal life. And he is fulfilling his promise to dwell in them.

It seems that John goes to extremes to make sure that his readers understand what he thinks the Holy Spirit is. The doors of the disciples' gathering place are locked so that no one can get in, and no one can get out. They are huddled together in fear. The risen Christ, the One into whom the Spirit has breathed new life, cannot be stopped by locked doors; he penetrates not only the doors of the house, but he also breaks into the very souls of his disciples by sharing and breathing the new life of the Holy Spirit into them. Reminiscent of the prophet Ezekiel's vision of dry bones which come alive by the power of the Spirit, Jesus resuscitates the lives of his followers.

We're no different than they. Many times in our lives have we needed Jesus to come and breathe the Spirit into us. When we are seriously ill, we need a good breath of Holy Spirit to heal us. After a spat, husbands and wives often seal their peace by sharing their spirits—nothing other than the Holy Spirit, of course—through a kiss. When he consecrates the Chrism Oil, the bishop may breathe over it to indicate that he is insufflating or breathing into it the Holy Spirit, who will be shared throughout his diocese when anyone or anything is anointed with it. A walk in the breeze filled with the perfume of various flowers can fill us with a new determination called the Holy Spirit.

So, as you pray this glorious mystery, reflect upon all the occasions in your life when Jesus has breathed the Holy Spirit into you. Notice how your locked doors were suddenly penetrated.

Option 3

Scripture: "When the day of Pentecost had come, [the twelve apostles] were all together in one place. And suddenly from heaven there came a sound like the rush of a violent wind, and it filled the entire house where they were sitting. Divided tongues, as of fire, appeared among them, and a tongue rested on each of them. All of them were filled with the Holy Spirit and began to speak in other languages, as the Spirit gave them ability." (Acts 2:1–4)

Reflection: The account of Pentecost in the Acts of the Apostles is one of Luke's best dramatic presentations woven from Hebrew Bible (Old Testament) imagery. Like the wind from God sweeps over the chaotic waters before creation, so does tornadic activity fill the house where the apostles are gathered; God is re-ordering worldly chaos. The fire of the burning bush encountered by Moses is now present in the flames resting on each apostle; every apostle shares Moses' theophanic light. And Babel, that Hebrew Bible (Old Testament) story explaining the origin of languages and why people could no longer communicate, is reversed, because now everyone can understand the apostles in his or her native tongue. Luke's narrative of the theophany of the Spirit even rivals that of the theophany at Mount Sinai (Horeb) when God gave the Torah to Moses.

Fifty days after Passover, now fifty days after Easter, the church is born, and out of the old Israel (the Jews) there emerges the new Israel (Christianity) which will be embraced by the Gentiles. The Spirit is the motivator and the animator which will open the church to the whole world, crossing all language barriers. Such is Luke's theological perspective.

While most of us have experienced the Holy Spirit in some form, probably not all—if any—of Luke's pyrotechnics were present, but the affects may have been the same. After being in a state of confusion or chaos, emerging into clarity of thought most likely was the work of the Holy Spirit. Discovering that you were filled with enthusiasm for a task or project may have been the Holy Spirit lighting a fire underneath of you. And we don't need to know another language to be able to speak in tongues. Sometimes not being able to communicate to another person verbally forces us to share in other ways, such as with our eyes, touch, smell, even pointing a finger here or there. That form of speech is certainly a manifestation of the Holy Spirit.

So as you pray this glorious mystery, reflect on the various ways the Holy Spirit has blown into your life, ordering your chaos, setting you on fire, and enabling you to share your thoughts with others.

Option 4

Scripture: "While Peter was . . . speaking, the Holy Spirit fell upon all who heard the word. The circumcised believers . . . were astounded that the gift of the Holy Spirit had been poured out even on the Gentiles . . . ." (Acts 10:44–45)

Reflection: Most people are not aware that, besides the first story of Pentecost in Acts 2:1–13, there is a second story of Pentecost later in the book. The first one is the Jewish Pentecost; the second is the Gentile Pentecost. The author of both accounts, Luke, is the first evangelist to develop an understanding of the Holy Spirit, theologically referred to as pneumatology. Luke declares that the Holy Spirit both launches and guides the missions of Jesus' apostles to the Jews and to the Gentiles.

Luke depicts the Jewish Pentecost as a theophany, a manifestation of God in wind, like creation; in fire, like Mount Sinai (Horeb); and in languages, like Babel, that occurs fifty days after Jesus' resurrection. While there is less fanfare in the account of the Gentile Pentecost, once the Spirit descends upon the centurion Cornelius and his household, all are baptized in the name of Jesus Christ.

Peter, as the representative of Jewish Christianity, cooperates with God through a series of visions to inaugurate the Gentile Pentecost. Once Peter reports to the rest of the apostles what the Mighty One is doing, it is not long before Luke introduces Saul (Paul) in the Acts. Paul picks up where Peter left off and becomes known as the apostle to the Gentiles. From chapter 13 on, the Acts of the Apostles narrates the activities of Paul among the Gentiles.

The metaphors for the Holy Spirit—wind, fire, and tongues—that worked for Luke continue for us today. The gathering of family and friends for birthdays, anniversaries, Thanksgiving, and Christmas remind all of the ties that bind them into one; there is a definite Spirit present as language discloses stories of suffering, tales of exploration, and narratives of experiences by young and old alike. A quiet walk in the park or woods might reveal a tree on fire with fall colors or the sunrise or sunset igniting the sky. A puff of air rattling the wind chimes may reveal the invisible presence of God's Spirit.

As you pray this mystery, reflect on some of your life's Pentecosts, those glorious Spirit-experiences of wind, fire, language, and breath.

The Assumption

Celebrated: August 15, The Assumption of the Blessed Virgin Mary

The Glorious Mysteries

Option 1

Scripture: "We know that our old self was crucified with [Christ] so that the body of sin might be destroyed, and we might no longer be enslaved to sin. For whoever has died is freed from sin. But if we have died with Christ, we believe that we will also live with him." (Rom 6:6–8)

Reflection: In his Letter to the Romans, Paul reflects upon the meaning of baptism, declaring that one is baptized into the death of Christ, buried with him, so that, just as Christ was raised from the dead by God, one might share newness of life. Thus, baptism destroys the body of sin, and the death undergone in its waters frees one from sin. When one re-emerges from the baptismal font, he or she is a new creation, living a new life.

Applied to the doctrine of the assumption of Mary into heaven, we can say that God baptized Mary before she was conceived in her mother's womb. The Holy One prepared her to be the mother of Jesus Christ. What God did for her, the Mighty One then accomplished for all through the death and resurrection of Christ. Our baptism into Christ's death and resurrection is our way of sharing in the sinless life of the Virgin Mary.

Furthermore, because she was without sin, God raised her from the dead, like he raised the only-begotten Son. The promise of our own resurrection one day, because of our baptism, is contained in our faith in the resurrection of Christ and his mother's assumption.

The dogma of the assumption of Mary gives us the opportunity to reflect upon our baptism, which, ideally, according to Paul, re-creates us. After having all our sins washed away through our death in the baptismal grave, we are raised from the watery womb to new life. Born again, we never have to sin another time. Because we have been incorporated into the body of Christ, we can live our new life sinless, already sharing resurrection, even while awaiting its fullness after physical death on the other side of the grave.

While the ideal is seldom achieved, it gives us a goal for which we strive. Paul urges us not to let sin dominate our mortal bodies in terms of our desires for food and drink, clothing, shelter, sex, etc. We can live as did the sinless Virgin of Nazareth because we have died in baptism and share in the divine life in which she was conceived.

As you pray this glorious mystery, reflect on all the ways you live your baptismal sinlessness and all the ways your desires lead you away from it.

Option 2

Scripture: ". . . [I]n fact Christ has been raised from the dead, the first fruits of those who have died. For since death came through a human being, the resurrection of the dead has also come through a human being." (1 Cor 15:20–21)

Reflection: The doctrine of the Virgin Mary's assumption into heaven, also referred to as the dormition, is not a biblical event. It can be understood only from the perspective of the doctrine of the Immaculate Conception, the belief that Mary was preserved free from all stain of original sin and from the belief that Jesus Christ, true God and true man, free of all sin, was raised from the dead by God. What is believed about Mary is based on what is believed about Christ. Thus, if Jesus is sinless and the Might One raised him from the dead, the logical conclusion is that Mary, his mother (the Mother of God), who was sinless, would also have been raised from the dead by the Holy One. The assumption of Mary is her participation in Christ's resurrection and serves as a foreshadowing of what awaits us, who follow her Son, on the other side of the grave.

In his First Letter to the Corinthians, Paul establishes the basis for this belief. He argues that there have been two Adams—the original one God created who sinned and brought death into the world and the second one, Christ, through whom God re-created and brought life into the world via the resurrection. Death brought by the first Adam has been defeated by the resurrection of the second Adam. Mary, the mother of the second Adam, is the second human being to experience resurrection because she, like her Son, was not subject to the death that was the result of the first Adam's disobedience. Thus, she has been assumed into heaven.

Mary's assumption represents what awaits us. She models what God can do in those who wait in faith, hope, and love for the Merciful One to act. You may be waiting for a new job or for a ride somewhere. You may be waiting for the birth of a child or the paperwork for an adoption to be completed. You may be waiting for a letter in the mail or a friend or family member to arrive for a visit. Any time that you wait in faith, hope, and love, you imitate Mary's waiting for God to act in her life. Her assumption is our guarantee that God raises to new life those who wait for the Holy One to act.

As you pray this mystery, reflect on the glorious deeds God has done in your life while you wait.

Option 3

Scripture: "So it is with the resurrection of the dead. What is sown is perishable, what is raised is imperishable. It is sown in dishonor, it is raised in glory. It is sown in weakness, it is raised in power. It is sown a physical body, it is raised a spiritual body. If there is physical body, there is also a spiritual body." (1 Cor 15:42–44)

Reflection: Mary's assumption into heaven is another way to speak about her resurrection. This non-biblical event can be understood theologically only by beginning with the sinless Christ, the Son of God, true God and true man, who was raised from the dead by the Mighty One. Mary is declared to be sinless from the moment of her immaculate conception because she was prepared by God to be the Mother of God. Therefore, just as the Holy One raised the sinless Christ from the dead, so would he raise sinless Mary from the dead.

Paul sets the stage for this doctrine in his First Letter to the Corinthians where he reflects on the meaning of the resurrection of the body. Death is the passageway to new life. After one dies, he or she is buried in the earth. That body is corruptible; what will be raised will be incorruptible. Death is a dishonor; resurrection is an honor. Death indicates that human beings are weak; resurrection bestows upon them power. Our physical bodies are born and die and are buried, but our spiritual bodies are raised for a completely different mode of existence.

Paul's teaching on the resurrection is illustrated in Mary's assumption. Because she was human, she died; metaphorically, she fell asleep. But her perishable, dishonorable, physical body was made imperishable, honorable, and spiritual by God. Because God had prepared her to be the mother of the Only-begotten Son, she has already shared in his resurrection.

What God did for Christ and for his mother, the Holy One has promised to do for us. Because of our faithfulness, God declares that our perishable, dishonorable, physical body will be rendered imperishable, honorable, and spiritual. In other words, just as we bear the image of the first Adam's corruption, so we shall bear the image of Christ's and his mother's incorruption.

As you pray this mystery, reflect on your own perishableness, the fact that you came into existence and that you will go out of existence. Also, reflect on your own imperishableness, the faith that God will raise you from the dead gloriously, like the Holy One raised his Son and his mother.

Option 4

Scripture: "Since, therefore, the children share flesh and blood, [Christ] himself likewise shared the same things, so that through death he might destroy the one who has the power of death, that is, the devil, and free those who all their lives were held in slavery by the fear of death." (Heb 2:14–15)

Reflection: The author of the Letter to the Hebrews understands flesh and blood as the humanity which Christ shared. Because Jesus was human, he shared in the fate of every human being: death. However, through his death, he defeated the devil, the one through whom death came into the world. In other words, death was not a part of God's original plan, so Jesus, through his ministry as the great high priest, restored the Mighty One's intention that people eat of the tree of life and live forever.

The dogma of the assumption of Mary states that the Virgin is the first, after Christ, to be restored to the Holy One's original plan. By the power of grace, the Mighty One anticipated what the Son would accomplish by preserving the young woman of Nazareth from sin. Because of her sinlessness, she was raised to new life, like her Son, who defeated death through his own resurrection. It was only fitting that she, a woman of flesh and blood, be assumed into heaven since death had no power over her.

We live in a death-denying culture. And because of that, most people have a great fear of death. People no longer die at home surrounded by members of their families. They are sent to hospitals or nursing homes to die. Death is a dirty word never to be spoken. Modern medicine has made it possible for people to prolong the death of a loved one for days, weeks, and years. Finally, when the death of a family member occurs, a crisis ensues, because we do not know how to die, how to let others die, and how to walk with those who are preparing to die.

The Letter to the Hebrews gives us hope. The power of death has been defeated by Christ's resurrection. The defeat of death is confirmed for us in Mary's assumption. There is nothing to fear; we no longer have to be slaves to a fear of death. We can continue our lifetime journey of faith that will end in death with the hope that what God did for Jesus and Mary, God will do for us.

As you pray this glorious mystery, surface your own fears of death and turn them into the hope that the assumption offers us.

The Coronation of Mary

Celebrated: August 22, The Queenship of the Blessed Virgin Mary

Option 1

Scripture: "When Jesus saw his mother and the disciple whom he loved standing beside her, he said to his mother, 'Woman, here is you son.' Then he said to the disciple, 'Here is your mother.' And from that hour the disciple took her into his own home." (John 19:26–27)

Reflection: Only John's Gospel portrays the mother of Jesus and the beloved disciple standing at the foot of the cross. Not only does the author of the Fourth Gospel never name the mother of Jesus, but he only puts her in two scenes: the crucifixion and the wedding at Cana. And in both scenes she seems to occupy special status.

At Cana it is the mother of Jesus who informs him that the newly-married couple has run out of wine. While he at first tells her that his hour has not yet come, she trusts that he will help the wedding reception by telling the servants to do whatever he tells them. At the cross, Jesus entrusts his mother to the disciple whom he loved, another unnamed character in John's Gospel, and entrusts him to his mother. Before the incarnate Word dies and completes his mission, he takes care of the one who enabled his coming into the world.

The mother of Jesus and the beloved disciple are portrayed by the author as ideal followers. Both see and believe. The mother of Jesus sees his first sign at Cana of Galilee and believes. The beloved disciple sees the empty tomb and believes. Throughout John's Gospel, people witness Jesus' signs and come to faith.

While the coronation of the Virgin Mary as queen of heaven is not a biblical story, it, nevertheless, exalts the mother of Jesus for her discipleship. As one believer, Jesus' mother exemplifies the trust of Christ that all of us need to have. As the other believer, the beloved disciple exemplifies the faith in Christ in whom all of us need to trust. By taking the mother of Jesus into his home, the beloved disciple furthers God's plan.

As you pray this glorious mystery, reflect upon all the ways that God continues the divine plan through you. Who are the unnamed people in your life—like the mother of Jesus and the disciple whom Jesus loved—who have made you aware of your part in God's plan?

Option 2

Scripture: "All these [eleven apostles] were constantly devoting themselves to prayer, together with certain women, including Mary the mother of Jesus, as well as his brothers." (Acts 1:14)

Reflection: In icons depicting Pentecost, usually Mary is seated at the top and the apostles are arranged six on either side of her. After the author of the Acts of Apostles—the same author who wrote Luke's Gospel—mentions that Mary joined the eleven in prayer, he narrates how a twelfth apostle, Matthias, was chosen to replace Judas. Then, he begins his story about Pentecost. Usually, icons depicting Pentecost show flames of fire coming to rest on the apostles and Mary seated with them. This is the only mention of the mother of Jesus in all of the twenty-eight chapters of the Acts.

But this one mention is enough for us to conclude that Mary, who was overshadowed by the power of the Most High God in the opening of Luke's Gospel, would also have to be present at the opening of the Acts of the Apostles to witness the outpouring of the Holy Spirit. It is also enough for us to conclude that she can be considered as the queen of the apostles, as she is often depicted in Pentecost icons.

Mary's crowning as queen of heaven is for the church. Not only does she aide the church's beginning with her prayers on earth, but after she is assumed into heaven and crowned as queen, she becomes a model of the church. In other words, by reflecting on the life of the Virgin Mary, all members of the church can find an image of faith to imitate. From her place in heaven she continues to help guide us on our pilgrim way. Thus, she is often spoken of as mother of the church

We might consider imitating her adherence to the Father's will; without hesitation she says yes to bearing the Son of the Most High. We might consider imitating her cooperation in her Son's work; she always points to him and ponders the events of his life in her heart. We might consider imitating her response to the Holy Spirit; she follows the plan marked out for her.

As queen of heaven, she awaits our arrival when we will one day be raised from the dead and assumed into heaven.

As you pray this glorious mystery, reflect on the ways that you can imitate Mary.

Option 3

Scripture: ". . . [W]hen the fullness of time had come, God sent his Son, born of a woman, born under the law, in order to redeem those who were under the law, so that we might receive adoption as children." (Gal 4:4–5)

The Glorious Mysteries

Reflection: While Paul does not mention Mary as the mother of Jesus in his Letter to the Galatians, he does refer to her as the woman who gave birth to him. As he also does in Romans, Paul presents his theological position that Jesus was born Jewish and incorporated into the covenant which was legislated by the Law or Torah. In Pauline understanding, Jesus redeemed all those under the burden of the Law; he set them free. He did not set them free for lawlessness, but he set them free from their attempts to earn salvation by keeping the Torah. Through Christ's establishment of a new covenant grounded in love, we are afforded the new status of adopted children of God.

When God decided that the time was right, Jesus was conceived in Mary and born. Through his death and resurrection, God has bought the freedom of all human beings and adopted them as the Holy One's children. Furthermore, just as God overshadowed Mary with the Holy Spirit, so the Mighty One has sent the Spirit into us, and that Spirit enables us to call upon God as our Father. Like Jesus, the Son of God, we become adopted children of God and heirs with Christ to eternal life.

The first person to share in the fullness of the freedom of a child of God was Mary. God anticipated what Christ would do and adopted her as his child before she was born. Thus, the fullness of time comes in the conception of the Virgin Mary and is continued through her conception of Jesus, her assumption into heaven, and her crowning as queen of heaven.

That same fullness of time is ours as the adopted children of God. Already, we are heirs of all that God has brought us through Christ. We share in God's grace, the very gift of the divine to us. We share in the Holy Spirit, who continues to unfold the divine plan in and through our lives lived in trust of God. We share in the freedom of the children of God through the sacraments of the church which draw us ever more closely to all other adopted brothers and sisters. The crowning glory of the Virgin Mary, an adopted daughter of God, awaits us when our pilgrimage here is ended.

As you pray this glorious mystery, reflect on how the fullness of time is manifested in your daily life.

Option 4

Scripture: "A great portent appeared in heaven: a woman clothed with the sun, with the moon under her feet, and on her head a crown of twelve stars." (Rev 12:1)

Reflection: Mary's exaltation and crowning by Christ as queen of heaven, like her assumption, is not a biblical event. It can be understood only from the perspective of the doctrine of the immaculate conception, the belief that Mary was preserved free from all stain of original sin, and from the doctrine of the assumption, that she was assumed body and soul into heaven. What is believed about Mary is based on what is believed about Christ. Thus, if Jesus is the king of kings through his resurrection from the dead by God, Mary, his mother, would have to be the queen through her assumption into heaven by the Mighty One. Thus, her coronation conforms the Mother of God even more closely to the image of Christ.

Apocalyptic literature, like that found in the Book of Revelation, attempts to depict this truth using a portent, a foreshadowing or omen written in signs or codes. The woman, the personification of Israel, from whom God brings forth the Messiah, is the incarnation of the dream of Jacob's son, Joseph, who sees the sun and moon and eleven stars bow to him. Israel is pregnant with and gives birth to the Messiah in the person of Mary of Nazareth, chosen by God from all eternity to be the mother of the Holy One's Son, Jesus Christ. Mary's coronation is the crowning of her absolute cooperation with God in the plan of salvation.

Even though today there are few royals, kings and queens, people look at them as a little above the commoners. We expect them to be above any ethical reproach. As contestants in beauty pageants, we want the winning queen to be flawless in poise, conversation, and song. What we look for in queens of any kind is what the Mighty One found in Mary, whom the Holy One selected to be the mother of God's own Son.

Through baptism, we, too, have been chosen. We are anointed, "Christed," with Chrism Oil and declared to be royal, chosen

The Glorious Mysteries

by God to cooperate with God in the plan of salvation. We exercise our royal status, like Mary, when we discern and affirm God's work in our lives.

As you pray this glorious mystery, reflect on your exercise of your royal status and look for traces of God's plan for your life.

Bibliography

Catechism of the Catholic Church. Washington, DC: United States Catholic Conference, 1994.
Catholic Source Book, The. Orlando, FL: Harcourt, 2007.
O'Day, Gail R. and David Peterson, eds. *The Access Bible: New Revised Standard Version with the Apocryphal/Deuterocanonical Books.* New York, NY: Oxford University Press, 1999.
Roman Missal, The: Study Edition. Collegeville, MN: Liturgical, 2012.
Scriptural Rosary, The. Glenview, IL: Christianica (America), 1961.

Recent Books by Mark G. Boyer

Nature Spirituality: Praying with Wind, Water, Earth, Fire

A Spirituality of Ageing

Caroling through Advent and Christmas: Daily Reflections with Familiar Hymns

Weekday Saints: Reflections on Their Scriptures

Human Wholeness: A Spirituality of Relationship

The Liturgical Environment: What the Documents Say (third edition)

A Simple Systematic Mariology

Praying Your Way through Luke's Gospel and the Acts of the Apostles

Daybreaks: Daily Reflections for Advent and Christmas

Daybreaks: Daily Reflections for Lent and Easter

An Abecedarian of Animal Spirit Guides: Spiritual Growth through Reflections on Creatures

Overcome with Paschal Joy: Chanting through Lent and Easter—Daily Reflections with Familiar Hymns

Taking Leave of Your Home: Moving in the Peace of Christ

A Spirituality of Mission: Reflections for Holy Week and Easter

Recent Books by Mark G. Boyer

An Abecedarian of Sacred Trees: Spiritual Growth through Reflections on Woody Plants

Divine Presence: Elements of Biblical Theophanies

Fruit of the Vine: A Biblical Spirituality of Wine

Names for Jesus: Reflections for Advent and Christmas

Talk to God and Listen to the Casual Reply: Experiencing the Spirituality of John Denver

Christ Our Passover Has Been Sacrificed: A Guide through Paschal Mystery Spirituality—Mystical Theology in The Roman Missal

www.ingramcontent.com/pod-product-compliance
Lightning Source LLC
Chambersburg PA
CBHW071449160426
43195CB00013B/2058